Updated 2018

Isis

The Divine Female

Expanded Edition

Moustafa Gadalla

Tehuti Research Foundation
International Head Office: Greensboro, NC, U.S.A.

Isis The Divine Female

by MOUSTAFA GADALLA

Published by:
Tehuti Research Foundation
P.O. Box 39491
Greensboro, NC 27438, U.S.A.

All rights reserved. No part of this book may be reproduced or transmitted in any form or by any means, electronic or mechanical, including photocopying, recorded or by any information storage and retrieval system without written permission from the author, except for the inclusion of brief quotations in a review.

Copyright 2016 and 2018 by Moustafa Gadalla, All rights reserved.

Publisher's Cataloging-in-Publication Data
Gadalla, Moustafa, 1944-
Isis The Divine Female / Moustafa Gadalla.
p. cm.
Includes bibliographical references.
Library of Congress Control Number: 2016900017

ISBN-13 (pdf): 978-1-931446-25-9
ISBN-13 (e-book): 978-1-931446- 26-6
ISBN-13 (pbk): 978-1-931446-31-0

1. Cosmology, Egyptian. 2. Egypt—Religion.3. Egypt—Religion—Influence 4. Gods, Egyptian.5. Occultism—Egypt 6. Science—Egypt—History. 7. Egypt—Civilization. 8. Christianity—Origin. 9. Egypt—History—To 640 A.D. I. Title.

CONTENTS

About the Author	vii
Preface	ix
Standards and Terminology	xiii
Map of Egypt and Surrounding Countries	xv
Chapter 1 : Isis: The Mother of Creation	1
1.1 Her Name	1
1.2 The Universal Womb	4
1.3 The One and All—Atam	7
1.4 Re: The Manifested Atam	10
1.5 Isis: The Image of Atam	11
1.6 Isis: The Female Re	12
1.7 Isis: The Dog Star	14
1.8 The Heart (Isis) Begets the Soul (Osiris)	15
Chapter 2 : The Duality of Isis [Isis and Nephthys]	19
2.1 The Duality of Divine Intellect	19
2.2 The Dual Nature of the Creation Cycle	20
2.3 The Dual Nature of the Universal Womb	21
2.4 The Two Ladies and The Diadem	23

Chapter 3 : Isis & Osiris—The Dynamic Duo — 25

3.1 Dualisms in Ancient Egypt — 25
3.2 Isis and Osiris as the Solar and Lunar Principles — 28
3.3 Isis and Osiris and the Four Elements of Creation — 29
3.4 The Societal Role of Isis and Osiris — 30

Chapter 4 : Isis: The Virgin Mother of 'God' — 33

4.1 Allegory and Fictional History — 33
4.2 Mary Isis — 34
4.3 Divine and Immaculate Conception — 35
4.4 The Virgin Mother of 'God' — 37
4.5 Mary Isis and Child Refuge Into Egypt — 37
4.6 The Divine Sacrifice — 38

Chapter 5 : The Numerology of Isis & Osiris — 41

5.1 The Primary Numbers of Isis and Osiris (2 & 3) — 41
5.2 The Primary Generating Numbers of Shapes and Forms — 43
5.3 The Musical Dynamo — 44
5.4 The Binary and Ternary Universal Rhythm — 46

Chapter 6 : Isis' Multitude of Attributes — 47

6.1 *Maat* — 48
6.2 *Seshat* — 58
6.3 *Net [Neith]* — 59
6.4 *Nut—Firmament* — 61
6.5 *Nephthys—Isis' Twin Sister* — 66
6.6 *Satet* — 67
6.7 *Ta-urt* — 67
6.8 *Mut* — 69
6.9 *Sekh-mut—The Den Mother* — 70
6.10 *Bast—The Docile Cat* — 72
6.11 *Qadesh* — 73
6.12 *Heqet* — 74
6.13 *Serket* — 75
6.14 *Anat* — 76
6.15 *Hathor—Venus* — 76

Chapter 7 : The Beloved in All Lands — 89

7.1 *The Spread of the Egyptian Religion* — 89
7.2 *Cosmic Significance of Egyptian Festivals* — 93
7.3 *Queen of Marshes* — 94
7.4 *Lady of Sorrow—[Cry Me A River]* — 96
7.5 *Isis: Lady of Assumption* — 99
7.6 *Celebrating Her 'Birthday'* — 101
7.7 *Celebrating Our (Holy) Mother of the Sea* — 101

Chapter 8 : The Mighty Heart — 105

8.1 *Mary Isis: The Cure-all* — 105
8.2 *Homage to the Queen* — 108

Appendix 1: Egyptian Cosmology and Allegories — 111

Appendix 2: The Universal Egyptian Allegory—Isis and Osiris — 113

Appendix 3: Heart and Soul—Metaphysical Reflections — 121

Glossary	125
Selected Bibliography	129
Sources and Notes	135
TRF Publications	141

ABOUT THE AUTHOR

Moustafa Gadalla is an Egyptian-American independent Egyptologist who was born in Cairo, Egypt in 1944. He holds a Bachelor of Science degree in civil engineering from Cairo University.

Gadalla is the author of twenty two published internationally acclaimed books about various aspects of Ancient Egyptian history and civilization and its influences worldwide.

He is the Founder and Chairman of the Tehuti Research Foundation (https://ww.egypt-tehuti.org)—an international, U.S.-based, non-profit organization dedicated to Ancient Egyptian studies. He is also the Founder and Head of the online Egyptian Mystical University (https://www.EgyptianMysticalUniversity.org).

From his early childhood, Gadalla pursued his Ancient Egyptian roots with passion, through continuous study and research. Since 1990, he has dedicated and concentrated all his time to researching and writing.

PREFACE

Unlike other books, this title will fill both the mind. with comprehensive information. as well as the heart, with a whole spectrum of emotions.

This book explains the divine female principle as the source of creation both metaphysically and physically; the relationship (and one-ness) of the female and male principles; offers an explanation of about twenty female deities as the manifestations of feminine attributes; considers the role of Isis' ideology throughout the world; and much more. This Expanded Edition of the book is divided into eight chapters and three appendices.

Chapter 1: **The Mother of Creation** covers Isis' role in the creation sequence, being an image of the totality of creation, and her relationship to Re and Osiris.

Chapter 2: **The Duality of Isis** covers her basic dual nature as the Divine Intellect as well as in the creation cycle and the universal womb.

Chapter 3: Isis & Osiris—The Dynamic Duo covers the combined roles of Isis and Osiris in the development and generation of all creations in the universe

***Chapter 4:** Isis: The Virgin Mother of 'God'* covers her role in the Divine immaculate Conception of her son Horus, the Virginity concept, her flight and refuge—together with her baby son—from the threats of the Evil force, and the sacrifice of her son's life.

***Chapter 5:** The Numerology of Isis & Osiris* covers the numbers of Isis and Osiris (being 2 and 3 – the Primary numbers of creation and growth) and how these two numbers generate all forms and shapes, musical harmonies, and the rhythms of the universe.

***Chapter 6:** Isis' Multitude of Attributes* covers sixteen female deities—being the manifestation of Isis as the female principle of the created universe.

***Chapter 7:** The Beloved in All Lands* covers the spread of Egyptian religion worldwide, how such beliefs live on in Christianity, and how Ancient Egyptian Isis' related religious festivals are being adopted by Christianity for Mary using the very same dates as the Egyptian calendar.

***Chapter 8:** The Mighty Heart* covers the eternal powerful impact of Isis on mankind as the seeker for comfort and cure-all.

***Appendix 1:** Allegory and Egyptian Cosmology* covers how well crafted allegories are the best—if not the only—way to covey complex subjects so that information is gained by all.

***Appendix 2:** The Universal Egyptian Allegory*—Isis and Osiris covers a shortened version of the story of the Isis and Osiris Egyptian allegory, with emphasis on the role of Isis as the divine female principle, manifestations and applications. The narrative is in broken segments, each followed by a concise metaphysical evaluation of each segment.

Appendix 3: *Heart and Soul—Metaphysical Reflections* covers the metaphysical aspects of the heart (Isis) and soul (Osiris) and how a human being is able to achieve integration of the heart and the soul within.

It should be noted that the digital edition of this book as published in PDF and E-book formats have a substantial number of photographs that compliment the text materials throughout the book.

Moustafa Gadalla

STANDARDS AND TERMINOLOGY

1. The Ancient Egyptian word neter and its feminine form netert have been wrongly, and possibly intentionally, translated to 'god' and 'goddess', by almost all academicians. Neteru (plural of neter/netert) are the divine principles and functions of the One Supreme God.

2. You may find variations in writing the same Ancient Egyptian term, such as Amen/Amon/Amun or Pir/Per. This is because the vowels you see in translated Egyptian texts are only approximations of sounds which are used by Western Egyptologists to help them pronounce Ancient Egyptian terms/words.

3. We will be using the most commonly recognized words for the English-speaking people that identify a neter/netert [god, goddess] or a pharaoh or city; followed by other 'variations' of such a word/term.

It should be noted that the real names of the deities (gods, goddesses) were kept secret so as to guard the cosmic power of the deity. The Neteru were referred to by epithets that describe particular qualities, attributes and/or aspect(s) of their roles. Such applies to all common terms such as Isis, Osiris, Amun, Re, Horus, etc.

4. When using the Latin calendar, we will use the following terms:

> **BCE** – Before Common Era. Also noted in other references as BC.
> **CE** – Common Era. Also noted in other references as AD.

5. The term Baladi will be used throughout this book to denote the present silent majority of Egyptians that adhere to the Ancient Egyptian traditions, with a thin exterior layer of Islam.[See *Ancient Egyptian Culture Revealed* by Moustafa Gadalla for detailed information.]

6. There were/are no Ancient Egyptian writings/texts that were categorized by the Egyptians themselves as "religious", "funerary", "sacred", etc. Western academia gave the Ancient Egyptian texts arbitrary names such as the "Book of This" and the "Book of That", "divisions", "utterances", "spells", etc. Western academia even decided that a certain "Book" had a "Theban version" or "this or that time period version". After believing their own inventive creation, academia accused the Ancient Egyptians of making mistakes and missing portions of their writings(?!!).

For ease of reference, we will mention the common but arbitrary Western academic categorization of Ancient Egyptian texts, even though the Ancient Egyptians themselves never did.

MAP OF EGYPT AND SURROUNDING COUNTRIES

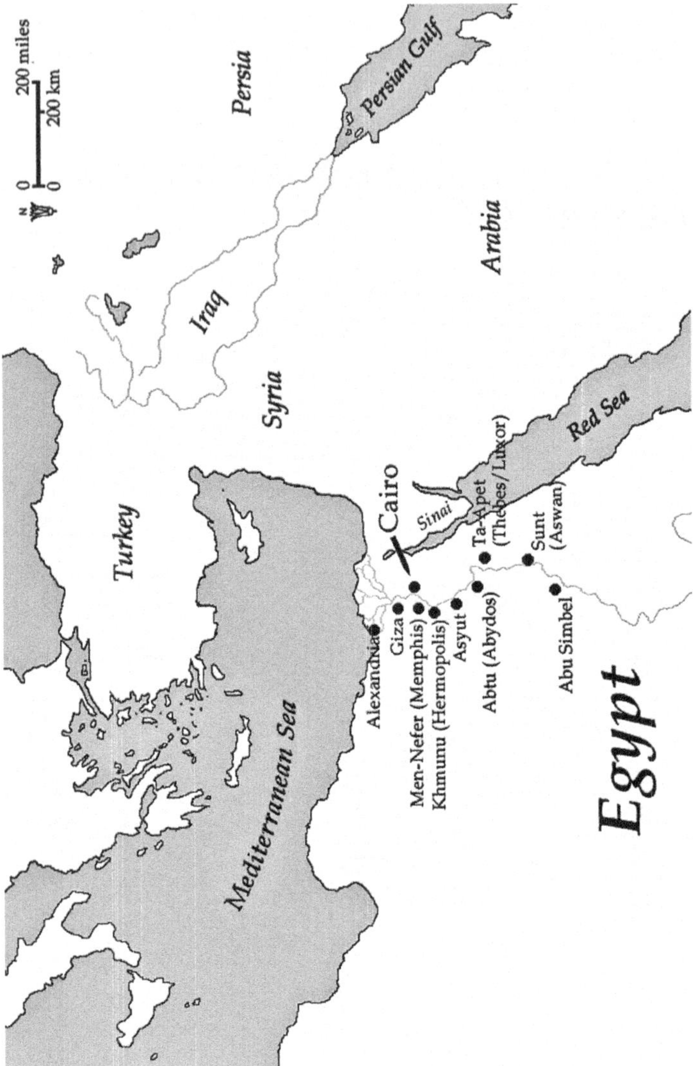

N
0 200 miles
0 200 km
Persian Gulf
Persia
Arabia
Iraq
Syria
Turkey
Mediterranean Sea
Red Sea
Sinai
Cairo
Alexandria
Giza
Men-Nefer (Memphis)
Khmunu (Hermopolis)
Asyut
Abtu (Abydos)
Ta-Apet (Thebes/Luxor)
Sunt (Aswan)
Abu Simbel
Egypt

CHAPTER 1 : ISIS: THE MOTHER OF CREATION

1.1 HER NAME

The present-day common use of the name Isis is limited to her aspect of maternal devotion, fidelity, and tenderness. But she is much more than that—she represents the divine female principle that includes the creative power that conceived (both physically and metaphysically) and brought forth all living creatures.

The Ancient Egyptians looked at Isis as the symbol of the cosmic feminine principle. This principle encompasses thousands of feminine qualities and attributes, and the Egyptians had terms to describe each manifestation of this feminine principle.

In the culture of English-speaking peoples, a *name* is merely a label to distinguish someone or something from another. But for the Egyptians (both the ancient and present-day silent majority), a common "name" represents the resume or synopsis of the qualities and attributes of an entity. Egyptian *common names* are the attributes and qualities of any entity. This will be similar to the English language words for carpenter, farmer, etc., which represent a specific activity.

In the English language, we refer to her *name* as Isis, but the Egyptians had a representative term that recognizes the totality of her cosmic feminine principle. This all-encompassing Egyptian word/term is **Auset**. So, what is in this Ancient Egyptian "name"? Let us look at the meanings of Auset, to demonstrate how a name represents qualities and attributes.

Auset consists of the main word **Aus** and the suffix **et**. Aus means *the source, the power*. In mathematics, we say 2 to the power of 2. This mathematical power is called *Aus*. The suffix 'et' at the end of Aus-et is a feminine ending.

In addition to **Aus** meaning *the source* and *the power*, it also means *the origin, the cause*.

In this regard, we will show Auset to be the source, power, and cause of the created universe, inclusive of everything within this universe.

Another interesting meaning for Au-set is **The Lady;** and indeed she is the Lady of Heaven and Earth. She represents the feminine principle in the universe. This principle manifests itself in different forms and ways, and therefore Isis was called, by the Ancient Egyptians, *Auset [Isis] of the 10,000 Names (meaning attributes)*.

Several words are derived directly from the Egyptian name Auset, such as **Seta**, which means the number 6. This is very significant because 6 is the ultimate number of space, volume, and time. The cube with its six surfaces is the model of earth. As such, she represents the universe's womb as well as Earth, as we will later discuss in detail.

Another related meaning to the name Auset is the English word '**seat**'. Isis is portrayed as always wearing a seat or throne on her head to symbolize her as the source of legitimacy, which is manifested in the Ancient Egyptian (as well as the present-day silent majority) adherence to the matrilineal and matriarchal society. This topic will be discussed later in this book.

As we have noted, the use of the common name in the English language of Isis hinders our comprehension of valuable information, knowledge, and wisdom. However, to make it easier for English-speaking readers, we will continue to use the word Isis and other Ancient Egyptian names familiar to the English language reader.

The role of Isis as the divine female principle in the Creation process has been recognized by all. She exists everywhere and has been known to all since time immemorial.

Plutarch made note of that in his *Moralia, Vol. V*:

> *"Isis is, in fact, the female principle of Nature, and is receptive of every form of generation, and by most people has been called by countless names, since, because of the force of Reason she turns herself to this thing*

or that and is receptive of all manner of shapes and forms."

To appreciate the roles of Isis **as the female principle** of nature, we must find her primary cosmic role in the orderly sequence of the Creation of the universe.

1.2 THE UNIVERSAL WOMB

Every Egyptian creation text begins with the same basic belief: that before the beginning of things, there was a liquidy primeval abyss everywhere; dark, endless, and without boundaries or directions. Egyptians called this cosmic ocean/watery chaos 'Nun' meaning non-existence; the nothingness that is the source of everything.

Scientists agree with the Ancient Egyptian description of the origin of the universe as being an abyss. Scientists refer to this abyss as 'neutron soup', where there are neither electrons nor protons, only neutrons forming one huge extremely dense nucleus. Such chaos, in the precreation state, was caused by the compression of matter – atoms did not exist in their normal states, but were squeezed so closely together that many atomic nuclei were crowded into a space previously occupied by a single normal atom. Under such conditions, the electrons of these atoms were squeezed out of their orbits and moved about freely in a chaotic, degenerate state.

This represented the un-polarized state of matter prior to the Big Bang.

The condensed energy in the pre-creation neutron soup was continuously building up, reaching an optimum concentration of energy that led to its explosion and expansion in what we describe as the Big Bang, about 15 billion years ago.

Expulsion forces, which cause all galaxies to move outwardly, are opposed by gravitational and contractional forces which pull galaxies together. At the present time, the outwardly- moving forces exceed the contractional forces, and therefore the limits of our universe are still expanding.

The expanding universe resulting from the Big Bang is like a huge bubble—or, better yet, it is a type of womb that contains the whole universe. This expanding universe is the womb that contains all creation. This is the womb of Isis, the universal mother of all.

Creation occurs when divine energy is born in a type of a womb which is represented by Isis. The womb has several manifestations. On the universal level, it is the space that contains the universe. It is also the womb of the mother, or the seeds planted in the soil—all these manifestations of the womb represent Isis.

Scientists tell us that at a certain point in time in the future, the universe will stop expanding and will start getting smaller. The microwave radiation from the Big Bang fireball (which is still rushing around) will start squashing down, heat up, and change color again until it becomes visible once more. The sky will become red and will then turn orange, yellow, and white, and will end in the *Big Crunch* where all matter and all radiation in the universe will come crashing together into one unit.

The *Big Crunch* is not the end by itself, for the reunited, crunched universe—neutron soup—will have the potential for a new creation called the *Big Bounce*.

This shows us that creation is basically a process that follows a basic cycle of birth-life-death and rebirth. We recognize that this cosmic cycle is the Big Bang, followed by life, followed by the Big Crunch; then we are again ready for a big bounce and a new creation cycle.

Not only does the whole universe follows this cycle, but man and other creatures follow this basic cycle, as well.

The main theme of all Ancient Egyptian texts is the perpetual cyclical nature of creation. So it is not surprising that the Ancient Egyptian texts, which described the Big Bang, have also described, in the usual Egyptian symbolic terms, The Big Crunch and the Big Bounce.

The Egyptian coffin texts (Spell 130) tells us that:

> *"After the millions of years of differentiated creation the mayhem before creation will return. Only the Complete One [Atam] and Aus-Ra will remain—no longer separated in space and time."*

The Ancient Egyptian text tells us two points. The first is the return of the created universe to mayhem at the end of the creation cycle, which signifies the Big Crunch. The second point is the potential for a new cyclical rebirth of the universe as symbolized by the presence of **Aus-Ra**.

As stated earlier, the word **Aus** means 'the power of'. As such, **Aus-Ra** means *the power of Ra [Re]*, meaning the *rebirth of Ra [Re]* the creation in the abyss of a pre-creation state.

The main theme of the Ancient Egyptian texts is the cyclical nature of creation: being born, living, dying, and regenerating again.

1.3 THE ONE AND ALL—ATAM

Creation came out of the state of no-creation. Such a state of the universe represents the Subjective Being—unformed, undefined, and undifferentiated energy/matter. Its inert energy is inactive.

On the other hand, the creation state is orderly, formed, defined, and differentiated. The totality of the divine energy during the creation state is called **Atam** by the Egyptians.

Atam means *the One-ness of all, the complete*. It is connected with the root '**tam**' or 'tamam', meaning *"to be complete" or "to make an end of"*.

In Ancient Egyptian texts, Atam means *this who completes or perfects*; and in the Litany of Re, Atam is recognized as *the Complete One, the ALL*.

Numerically, one is not a number, but the essence of the underlying principle of number; all other numbers being made of it. One represents Unity: the Absolute as unpolarized energy. Atam as the number One is neither odd nor even, but both. It is neither female nor male, but both.

Atam is the totality of the orderly energy matrix during the creation stage, while Nun is the disorderly energy compound—the Subjective Being. The total divine energy within the universe is called Nun in its mayhem state and Atam in its orderly creation state/process.

Atam represents the release, in an orderly sequence, of the existing energy within Nun, bringing it to life. This represents the Objective Being.

The Divine energy that manifests itself in the creation cycle is defined by its constituent energy aspects, which were called neteru by the Ancient Egyptians. In order for creation to exist and to be maintained, this divine energy must be thought of in terms of male and female principles. Therefore, Ancient Egyptians expressed the cosmic energy forces in the terms of *netert* (female principle) and *neter* (male principle).

The Egyptian word *neter* (or nature or *netjer*) means a power that is able to generate life and to maintain it when generated. As all parts of creation go through the cycle of birth-life-death-rebirth, so do the driving energies, during the stages of this cycle. It is therefore that the Ancient Egyptian neteru, being divine energies, went (and continue to go) through the same cycles of birth-growth-death and renewal. Such understanding was common to all, as noted by Plutarch: that the multitude forces of nature known as neteru are born or created, subject to continuous changes, age and die, and are reborn. When you think of neteru not as gods and goddesses but as cosmic energy forces, one can see the Ancient Egyptian system as a brilliant representation of the cosmos.

Atam, The Master of the Cosmos is recognized in the Ancient Egyptian texts as *the complete one who contains all*. The Ancient Egyptian text reads:

> *"I am many of names and many of forms, and my Being exists in every neter* [god, goddess]*".*

The seed of creation out of which everything originated is Atam. And, just as the plant is contained within the seed, so everything that is created in the universe is Atam, too.

Atam, the One who is the All, as the Master of the Universe, declares, in the Ancient Egyptian papyrus commonly known as the *Bremner-Rhind Papyrus*:

> *"When I manifested myself into existence, existence existed.*
> *I came into existence in the form of the Existent, which came into existence in the First Time.*
> *Coming into existence according to the mode of existence of the Existent, I therefore existed.*
> *And it was thus that the Existent came into existence."*

In other words, when the Master of the Universe came into existence, the whole creation came into existence because the Complete One contains the all. All Ancient Egyptian texts reflect this sophisticated thought, emphasizing a progressive and orderly sequence of creation.

Creation is the sorting out (giving definition to/bringing order to) of all the chaos (the undifferentiated energy/matter and consciousness) of the primeval state. All Ancient Egyptian accounts of creation exhibited this with well defined, clearly demarcated stages.

The first stage of creation was represented by the Egyptians as Atam/Atum/Adam emerging out of Nu/Ny/Nun—the neutron soup.

Throughout the Ancient Egyptian texts, we consistently find how one state of being develops (or better yet, emerges) into the next state of being. And we always find that any two consecutive states are images of each other. Not only is that scientifically correct; but it is orderly, natural, and poetic. The Egyptians were famous for writing these scientific and philosophical subjects in poetic forms.

1.4 RE: THE MANIFESTED ATAM

Atam represents the realization of the total cosmic existence.

The role of Re in the creation process is best described in chapter 17 of the ancient Egyptian *Book of the Coming Forth by Light*—which is erroneously still called the *Book of the Dead* – where we learn that Re is the primeval cosmic creative force, the manifestation of Atam.

In the Egyptian text, Atam states:

> *"I appeared as Re on the eastern horizon of heaven..."*

Another version in this ancient Egyptian book reads:

> *"I am Atam (the All) when I was alone in the Watery Abyss.*
> *I am Re in his manifestations...".*

Re represents the primeval, cosmic, creative force; the manifestation of A-tam.

When Atam is combined with Re (the creative force), the resultant is Re-Atam, representing the manifestation of the creative force.

1.5 ISIS: THE IMAGE OF ATAM

We have seen how an orderly creation in the form of Atam, the Complete One emerged out of the pre-creation chaotic state of the Nun—the nothingness.

We have also seen how one state of being develops or emerges into the next state of being, and how every two consecutive stages are images of each other. Nun and Atam are images of each other, like the numbers 0 and 1—0 is nothing, nil, and 1 means the all.

The first thing that developed from the light of unity of the Complete One was the force of Active Reason, as He made two arise from one, by repetition.

This divine active reason thought is the first 'thing' of whom existence may proceed as the act, offspring, and image of the first—Atam. The ability to conceive—both mentally and physically—was naturally represented by the female principle Isis, being the feminine side of Atam's unity. This was confirmed plainly in Plutarch's writings, where he wrote in his *Moralia, Vol. V*:

> *"... since, because of the force of Reason. Isis turns herself to this thing or that and is receptive of all manner of shapes and forms."*

It is Isis being this Divine-Mind or Divine-Intellection, or Divine-Intellectual-Principle which begins the existence of Plurality, or Complexity, or Multiplicity.

The relationship between the master of the universe—The Complete One—and the mother of creation is best described in musical terms. The relationship between Atam the Complete One and his female image (being Isis) is like the relationship between a sound of a note and its octave note. Consider a string of a given length as unity. Set it vibrating, and it produces a sound. Stop the string at its midpoint and set it vibrating. The frequency of vibrations produced is double that given by the whole string, and the tone is raised by one octave. The string length has been divided by two, and the number of vibrations per second has been multiplied by two: one half (1:2) as created its mirror opposite (2:1), 2/1. This harmonic relationship is represented by Atam and Isis.

Isis' number is two, which symbolizes the power of multiplicity; the female mutable receptacle, horizontal, representing the basis of everything. In Ancient Egyptian thinking, Isis as the number two is the image of the first principle—the divine intellect.

1.6 ISIS: THE FEMALE RE

The relation of the intellect to the Complete One, Atam, is like the relation of the light of the sun effusing from the sun. The Ancient Egyptian texts describe Isis as being the divine sunshine, for she is called:

> *The daughter of the universal Lord.*
> *The female Re.*
> *The Light-giver in heaven with Re.*

Isis, then, is the emanated energy from the Complete One. As the female principle in the universe, only she can conceive and deliver the created universe.

In other words, Isis is the image of the cosmic creative

impulse, recognized by the term 'Re'. Thus, when speaking of Re, the Ancient Egyptian text says:

"Thou art the bodies of Isis."

This implies that Re, the creative energy, appears also in the different aspects of the cosmic female principle Isis. As such, Isis is recognized as:

The female Re.
The Lady of the beginning of time.
The prototype of all beings.
The greatest of the neteru—[meaning the divine forces].
The Queen of all the neteru.

Isis is recognized in the Ancient Egyptian texts as the God-Mother. How loving Isis is—our God-Mother. She (the female principle) is the matrix of the created universe (matrix being a motherly term; 'mater-x').

Isis, being the replicated image of the totality of creation, is the one who contains all creatures. Once again, in musical terms, we find that between the original note (produced from the whole length—*Do*) and the sound (produced at the half point, its octave—*Do*1), there are six positions where the ear interprets six different harmonious sounds (*Re, Mi, Fa, Sol, La, Si*), located at unequal distances from each other. The reaction to all the sounds of natural tones is characterized by an unmistakable sense of equilibrium. This sense of balance and harmony is governed by one of Isis' female manifestations—known as Maat.

1.7 ISIS: THE DOG STAR

During very remote periods of Ancient Egyptian history, Isis was associated with the star Sirius, the brightest star in heaven, which was called (like her) *the Great Provider*. Egypt's ingenious and very accurate calendar was based on the observation and study of Sirius' movements in the sky.

Numerous monuments can be found throughout Ancient Egyptian sites, attesting to their full awareness and knowledge of cosmology and astronomy. A systematic kind of astronomical observation began in Ancient Egypt at a very early time. The Ancient Egyptians compiled information, making charts of the constellations based on observations and recordings of Sirius and *the star that follows Sirius*.

The Greeks, Romans, and other ancient sources affirmed that the Egyptians regarded Sirius as the great central fire about which our solar system orbits. Sirius' movements are intimately associated with another companion star. Sirius and its companion are revolving around their common center of gravity or, in other words, revolving about each other. Sirius' diameter is less than twice the diameter of our sun. Its companion, however, has a diameter only about three times the diameter of Earth; yet it weighs about 250,000 times as much as the Earth. Its material is packed together so tightly that it is about 5,000 times as dense as lead. Such a compression of matter means that Sirius' companion's atoms do not exist in their normal states, but are squeezed so closely together that many atomic nuclei are crowded into a space previously occupied by a single normal atom; i.e. the electrons of these atoms are squeezed out of their orbits and move about freely (in a degenerate state). This is the Egyptian Nun; the neutron soup—the origin of all matter and energy in the universe.

The movement of Sirius' companion on its own axis and around Sirius upholds all creation in space; and, as such, is considered the starting point of creation. Ancient Egyptian records state that the commencement of the Sothic period corresponded with the beginning of the world—the beginning of a zodiac cycle of about 26,000 years.

1.8 THE HEART (ISIS) BEGETS THE SOUL (OSIRIS)

Now, with the plan of creation being conceived in the Divine Reason, the next logical step is to bring it to life. Therefore, Isis the Divine-Thinking engenders a power appropriate to the realization of its Thought. The bringing to life or animation of the creation plan is brought on by the All Soul, or Universal Soul of the All. The universal soul was represented in Ancient Egypt by Osiris, the third in the sequence of creation, and the number 3 was communicated through him. Osiris is the eternal emanation and image of the Second Hypostasis, the Intellectual-Principle.

Every stage of creation tends to engender an image of itself. It tends also to rejoin the next highest, of which it is itself a shadow or lower manifestation—for Isis is an image of the first principle and her shadow is Osiris. How enlightening!

In the orderly sequence of creation, it was the female

principle Isis who, after conceiving the plan, gave life to it. As such, Isis is called:

> *Isis, the Bestower of Life.*
> *Isis, the Lady of Life.*
> *Isis, the Giver of Life.*
> *Isis, the dweller in Neteru.*

Isis is the bestower of the universal life force—being Osiris.

Isis and Osiris are also mirror images of each other (or, in other words, the female and male are mirror images of each other).

On an intellectual level, the female principle is both passive and active; for Isis conceives the plan in a passive mode and then provides life to the plan, thus reflecting her activeness as an extension of her passiveness – i.e., the intellect and world soul stand in relation to an active and passive intellect.

Intellect is as it is: always the same, resting in a static activity. This is a feminine attribute. Movement towards it and around it is the work of Soul, proceeding from Intellect to Soul and making Soul intellectual; not making another nature between Intellect and Soul.

And on the soul level, Isis is the passive soul and Osiris is the active soul.

Again and again, we find the sequence of creation is based on one stage being the natural progression as well as the image of the following stage—and in reverse. From active-passive to passive-active is the chain reaction (so to speak) of creation.

Time is presented as the 'life' of the Soul, in contrast to Eternity, which is the mode of existence of Intellect. However, Soul is an entity that spans various levels of reality, and we find, on occasion, the highest aspect, at least, of Soul largely assimilated to intellect.

The relation of the soul to the intellect is like the relation of the light of the moon to the light of the sun. Just as when the moon becomes full from the light of the sun, its light becomes an imitation of the light of the sun in the same way. When the soul receives the effusion from the intellect, its virtues become perfect and its acts imitate acts of the intellect. When its virtues become perfect, then it knows its essence or self and the reality of its substance.

The combined forces of the divine mind and divine soul make the creation of the natural world possible. Isis as the Divine-Intellectual-Principle has two Acts—that of upward contemplation of The One, and that of 'generation' towards the lower All Soul. Likewise, the All-Soul has two Acts: it at once contemplates the Intellectual Principle and 'generates' in the bounty of its own perfection the Nature-Looking and Generative Soul, whose operation it is to generate or fashion the lower, material Universe upon the model of the Divine-Thoughts and the 'Ideas' laid up within the Divine-Mind. The All-Soul is the mobile cause of movement as well as of Form or material or a sense-grasped Universe, which is the Soul's Act and emanation, image and 'shadow'.

With the combined forces of female and male energies, the creation plan can come to life.

CHAPTER 2 : THE DUALITY OF ISIS [ISIS AND NEPHTHYS]

2.1 THE DUALITY OF DIVINE INTELLECT

Earlier, we found that the intellectual powers of Isis led to the conception and creation of the animated soul that we call Osiris. But duality also exists in the intellectual realm of Isis, whose symbolic number is 2 and its multiplications.

The dual complimentary nature of intellect lies in its ability to analyze what is followed, or to lead to the ability to reconcile. This dual nature of intellect was symbolized by the two sisters Isis and Nephthys. Isis and Nephthys are portrayed as "sisters" to highlight their numerous dual symbolism/activities.

Isis is represented by the cobra, while Nephthys is represented by the vulture.

The mighty cobra, which can swallow a huge animal and digest it, was, for Egyptians, the earthly manifestation of the divine intellect. The faculty of intellect allows a person to break down a whole (complex issue/body) into its constituent parts, in order to digest it.

The intellectual symbolism of the cobra is complimented by the vulture's primordial reconciliation. Reconciliation is also a feminine aspect of the universe.

Intellect requires the ability to analyze (break up) and reconcile and assimilate.

2.2 THE DUAL NATURE OF THE CREATION CYCLE

The two female deities Isis and Nephthys appear together in numerous places in the Egyptian records. They are always almost depicted together, and very rarely are depicted individually.

They may be considered Twin Sisters—or better yet, the dual nature of the female principle.

In the tomb of Queen Nefertari, we find the rejuvenated green solar deity in a mummiform body.

On the right, by Isis, we read:

This is Re who comes to rest in Osiris.

On the left, by Nephthys, we read:

> *This is Osiris who comes to rest in Re.*

Egyptian texts refer to Re and Osiris as **The Twin Souls.**

The two male deities of Re and Osiris have a counterpart in the dual female nature of the creation cycle, namely **The Twin Sisters**.

2.3 THE DUAL NATURE OF THE UNIVERSAL WOMB

On the cosmic level, Isis represents multiplication, fertility, and enlarging the womb of a mother or the huge, enlarging bubble that we call the universe. Her sister Nephthys ensures orderly and harmonic expansion by establishing outer boundaries or limitations on expansion. They both ensure an orderly expansion and contraction (divine energies) between the Big Bang and the Big Crunch.

On the universal level, Isis represents the active expanding womb that is called the universe, and her twin sister Nephthys represents the outer limits or perimeter of the universal bubble.

The twin sisters are mirror images of each other. Isis represents the part of the world that is visible, while Nephthys represents that which is invisible.

Isis and Nephthys represent, respectively, the things that are and the things that are yet to come into being; the beginning and the end, birth and death, life and death.

Isis symbolizes birth, growth, development and vigor. Nephthys represents death, decay, diminution and immobility. Nephthys represents death, and is associated with the coming into existence of the life that springs from death. Isis and Nephthys were, however, inseparably associated with each other, and in all the important matters which concern the welfare of the deceased, they acted together and appear together in bas-reliefs and vignettes.

Since As Above So Below, the dual action of the two sisters on the cosmic level are found on Earth, and one of their dual manifestations is their representation of fertility of the Land of Egypt.

Isis represents the fertile portions of Earth, while her sister, Nephthys, represents the barren perimeter of fertility. In his *Moralia, Vol. V*, Plutarch explained it:

> . . .the Egyptians hold and believe the earth to be the body of Isis, not all of it, but so much of it as the Nile covers, fertilizing it and uniting with it. . . The outmost parts of the land beside the mountains and bordering on the sea the Egyptians call Nephthys. This is why they give to Nephthys the name of "Finality".

Isis, in several of her 10,000 names, is called:

> **Creatress of green things.**

Green goddess, whose green color is like unto the greenness of the earth.
Lady of abundance.
Lady of Green Crops.
The Green Netert (Uatchet).

At the end of the green areas that are full of life is Nephthys, whose name, 'finality', means *complete, conclusive, settled*.

2.4 THE TWO LADIES AND THE DIADEM

The twin sisters had a major role in king-making. In one of the many attributes of Isis, she is called:

The Maker of Kings.
Isis, who delivereth to the king his rank, without whom no king can exist.

In the Ancient Egyptian texts, the King declares that he owes his sovereignty to the favor of the Sisters Pair, Isis and Nephthys. Their symbolic representations are found on the famous diadems worn by the Egyptian Pharaohs.

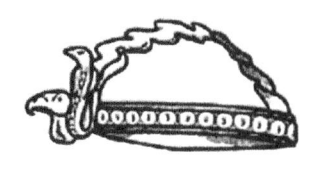

One of the Egyptian King's titles was *Lord of the diadem of the vulture and of the serpent*. The diadem, combining the serpent and vulture, was the earthly symbol of the divine man, the King. The diadem consisted of the serpent (a symbol of the divisive intellectual function) and the vulture (a symbol of the reconciliation function). The divine man must be able both to distinguish and to reconcile. Since these dual powers reside in man's brain, the form of the serpent's body follows the actual physiological sutures of the brain in which these particularly human faculties are seated.

Located in the middle of the forehead, the diadem represents the third eye, with all its metaphysical powers.

CHAPTER 3 : ISIS & OSIRIS—THE DYNAMIC DUO

3.1 DUALISMS IN ANCIENT EGYPT

The world, as we know it, is held together by a law that is based on the balanced dual nature of all things (wholes, units). Among noticeable polarized pairs are: male and female, odd and even, negative and positive, active and passive, light and darkness, yes and no, and true and false. Each pair represents a different aspect of the same fundamental principle of polarity, and each aspect partakes of the natures of unity and duality.

The most eloquent expression of the dual nature is present in the Ancient Egyptian text, known as the *Bremner-Rhind Papyrus*:

> *"I was anterior to the Two Anteriors that I made, for I had priority over the Two Anteriors that I made, for my name was anterior to theirs, for I made them anterior to the Two Anteriors..."*

The universal dual nature of creation manifests itself in various applications, as identified in Ancient Egypt.

Each dualizing aspect of the creation process is represented by two divine attributes or neteru. Depending on each specific aspect, the dualizing neteru may be:

- A female and a male
- 2 females
- 2 males
- 2 halves of unisex

Several duals were utilized in Ancient Egypt so as to correspond to the various situations. A very brief overview of sample Egyptian applications are shown here, for three areas:

A. Creation—Formative Aspects

a – Shu and Tefnut—represent the initial action of creation forming the universal bubble
b – Isis and Nephthys expands & contracts the universal bubble
c – Isis and Osiris represent the action within the universal bubble

B. Unification Aspects—[Tying The Knot]

a – Horus and Thoth
b – Two Hapis [Unisex]
c – Qareens of the Two Lands

C. Cyclical Aspects

a – Osiris and Horus
b – Re and Osiris
c – Aker

The dual **Shu** and **Tefnut** represent the initial action of creation. The created universe is subject to two opposing forces:

> 1. The expulsion forces, which cause all galaxies to move away from us. **Shu** represents this force. He symbolizes the heat and air—a male aspect of the universe rising and expanding.
>
> 2. The opposing force to expulsion and expansion is a contractional force which pulls the galaxies together. **Tefnut** symbolizes this contraction force—a female aspect of the universe to bring things together (the Den Mother).

Isis and Osiris are the dynamic dual that regulates the action within the universal bubble that contains all creation.

The most significant aspects of this duality are best described by Diodorus of Sicily, who wrote in his book, *Volume I*:

> ***Isis and Osiris hold, regulate the entire universe, giving both nourishment and increase to all things . . Moreover, practically all the physical matter which is essential to the generation of all things is furnished by these two. . .***

Here we will show some manifestations of the interplay between the female and male principles of Isis and Osiris, such as the permanence of the female principle and the temporal, changing, and cyclical male principle as applied to the

– Solar and Lunar Principles

- Four elements of creation
- Societal Role of Isis and Osiris

3.2 ISIS AND OSIRIS AS THE SOLAR AND LUNAR PRINCIPLES

The significance and interplay between solar and lunar principles is symbolized by the sun and moon.

The sun and the moon, among other things related to Isis and Osiris, are best described by Diodorus of Sicily, *Book I, 11. 5-6*:

> *These two neteru (gods), they hold, regulate the entire universe, giving both nourishment and increase to all things...*
>
> *Moreover, practically all the physical matter which is essential to the generation of all things is furnished by these two neteru (gods), <u>Isis and Osiris, symbolized as the sun and the moon.</u> The sun contributing the fiery element and the spirit, the moon the wet and the dry, and both together the air; and it is through these elements that all things are engendered and nourished. And so it is out of the sun and moon that the whole physical body of the universe is made complete; and as for the five parts just named of these bodies—the spirit, the fire, the dry, as well as the wet, and, lastly, the air-like—just as in the case of a man we enumerate head and hands and feet and the other parts, so in the same way the body of the universe is composed in its entirety of these parts.*

Diodorus' statements highlight:

1. The Egyptian concept that the neteru (gods, goddesses) are the forces of nature and not actual characters.
2. The importance of the four elements of creation.
3. The fact that human body is a miniature universe.

So the archetypal model of solar and lunar principles is based on the fact that all aspects of the universe follow this criteria of an original and permanent female principle and a cyclical, changeable, and moving male principle. The female is the sun—the source of energy – and the male principle is the moon that manifests/reflects this energy in the universe.

3.3 ISIS AND OSIRIS AND THE FOUR ELEMENTS OF CREATION

Of the four elements of creation—earth, water, air, and fire – the element that is solid and permanent is earth.

Several of Isis' 10,000 names relate to her being Mother Earth:

> *The Queen of earth.*
> *Lady of the solid earth.*

The four elements of the world (water, fire, earth, and air) were described by Plutarch in his *Moralia, Vol. V*:

> *"The Egyptians simply give the name of Osiris to the whole source and faculty creative of moisture, believing this to be the cause of generation and the substance of life-producing seed; and the name of Seth they give to all that is dry, fiery, and arid, in general, and antagonistic to moisture.*

> *As the Egyptians regard the Nile as the effusion of Osiris, so they hold and believe the earth to be the body of Isis, not all of it, but so much of it as the Nile covers, fertilizing it and uniting with it. From this union they make Horus to be born. The all-conserving and fostering Hora, that is the seasonable tempering of the surrounding air, is Horus.*
>
> *The insidious scheming and usurpation of Seth, then, is the power of drought, which gains control and dissipates the moisture which is the source of the Nile and of its rising."*

So, while Isis, the divine female principle, represents solid earth, the other three elements are representations of the changeable male principle.

Osiris is the water which comes and goes, rises during floods and high tide, and recedes and evaporates totally, disppearing to rise again in a new cycle.

Horus is the air, moving and shifting, which rises when it warms up and falls when it cools down.

Seth is the fire, moving and causing droughts.

3.4 THE SOCIETAL ROLE OF ISIS AND OSIRIS

As stated above, Isis represents the sun and her husband Osiris represents the moon. The light of the moon (Osiris) is a reflection of the light of the sun (Isis).

The Ancient Egyptian social/political system complies with the relationship between the sun (female) and the moon (male). As a result, this social/political law was reflected in the Egyptian allegory of Osiris, who became the Pharaoh of Egypt as a result of his marrying Isis.

Isis, in Egyptian, means 'seat/throne' (i.e. authority), and is the principle of legitimacy. It is therefore that Isis is always shown wearing a throne upon her head. Isis did not represent the "woman behind the throne", but the throne itself.

The throne of Isis represents the principle of legitimacy as a female-based (feminine) principle. In Egypt, the significance of Isis as the seat/authority/legitimacy was the basis for Egypt's adoption of the matrilineal/matriarchal principle in their society.

The role of the feminine principle Isis in the societal order is shown in several of her 10,000 names; for she is called, among other things:

> **The Maker of Kings.**
> **Who delivereth to the king his rank, without whom no king can exist.**

Throughout Egyptian history, it was the queen who transmitted solar blood. The queen was the true sovereign, landowner, keeper of the royalty, and guardian of the lineage's purity. A man who married the eldest Egyptian princess claimed a right to the throne. Through marriage, she transmitted the crown to her husband-he only acted as her executive agent.

The Pharaohs, as well as the leaders of smaller localities, adhered to this system. If the Pharaoh/leader had no daughters, a dynasty ended and a new dynasty began, with a new revered maiden as a seed for a new dynasty.

Matrilineal practices also applied to the whole society, as is evident from the funerary stelae of all kinds of people, where it is the usual custom to trace the descent of the deceased on the mother's side and not on that of the father. The person's mother is specified; but not the father – or, he is only incidentally mentioned. This tradition is still enduring secretly among the *Baladi* Egyptians, the silent majority in Egypt.

Even English (and practically all European languages) has the matrilineal principle in their structured words. The word *family* is etymologically centered around the female; for the female is the heart of the family.

CHAPTER 4 : ISIS: THE VIRGIN MOTHER OF 'GOD'

4.1 ALLEGORY AND FICTIONAL HISTORY

The very thing that is now called the Christian religion was already in existence in Ancient Egypt long before the adoption of the New Testament. The British Egyptologist Sir E. A. Wallis Budge wrote in his book *The Gods of the Egyptians* [1969]:

> *"The new religion (Christianity) which was preached there by St. Mark and his immediate followers, in all essentials so closely resembled that which was the outcome of the worship of Osiris, Isis, and Horus."*

The similarities noted by Budge and everyone who has compared the Egyptian Osiris/Isis/Horus allegory to the Gospel story, are striking. Both accounts are practically the same, e.g. the supernatural conception, the divine birth, struggles against the enemy in the wilderness, and the resurrection from death to eternal life. The main difference between the "two versions" is that the Gospel tale is considered historical and the Osiris/Isis/Horus cycle is an allegory.

Allegories are intentionally chosen as a means for communicating knowledge. Allegories dramatize cosmic laws, principles, processes, relationships and functions, and express them in a way easy to understand. Once the inner meanings of allegories have been revealed, they become marvels of simultaneous scientific and philosophical completeness and conciseness. The more they are studied, the richer they become. The 'inner dimension' of the teachings embedded into each story make them capable of revealing several layers of knowledge according to the listener's stage of development. The "secrets" are revealed as one evolves higher. The higher we get, the more we see. It is always there.

The Egyptians did not believe their allegories to be historical facts. They believed IN them, in the sense that they believed in the truth beneath the stories. The real power of the story/allegory lies in its ability to transform the life of every individual.

The biblical stories have completely mutilated the Ancient Egyptian allegories. The Christian religion threw away and lost the very soul of their meaning when they mistranslated the Ancient Egyptian allegorical language into alleged history, instead of viewing it as spiritual allegory. The result was a pathetic, blind faith in a kind of emotional and superstitious supernaturalism which effectively aborted the real power of the story/allegory to transform the life of every individual.

4.2 MARY ISIS

Throughout Ancient Egyptian texts, Isis is called 'Mary Isis'.

The origin of the word Mary lies in Ancient Egypt, where the written word was MR (the vowels a and y were added by modern scholars to help pronounce the ancient language), meaning **the beloved**.

The word Mary/Mery is one of the most repeated words in Ancient Egyptian texts. It was used as an adjective (epithet) before the names of people, neteru (gods, goddesses), etc.

Likewise, we find that the name Mary is given to many women in the Bible.

The two closest women to Jesus were called Mary: his mother, and Mary Magdalene.

4.3 DIVINE AND IMMACULATE CONCEPTION

The concept of the birth of the Messiah without sexual intercourse originated in Ancient Egypt. Isis is said to have conceived her son Horus after her husband Osiris' death.

The cosmic force responsible for her impregnation was MeSSeH., the crocodile star, as per Spell 148 of the Coffin Texts:

> ***"The crocodile star (MeSSeH) strikes . . . Isis wakes pregnant with the seed of Osiris—namely Horus."***

The English word Messiah originated also from the Hebrew and Aramic Mashih which, in its form as a verb MeSHeH., means 'to anoint'. This word is of Egyptian origin, whereas MeSSeH [the letter s in Egyptian is equivalent to sh in Hebrew and Aramaic] signified the ritual of anointing Ancient Egyptian Kings with the fat of crocodiles, as was the tradition with all kings in Ancient Egypt since at least 2700 BCE.

Anointing was a ritual of the coronation of the Egyptian King. Thus, the Christ/Messiah means 'the anointed one', who is the king.

That Isis was able to conceive without male impregnation after the death of her husband was a story embedded in Ancient Egypt since its most remote times.

Divine Conception is found in the oldest recovered findings in Ancient Egypt more than 5,000 years ago.

The Egyptian way of thinking about Divine Conception affirms that it was an Immaculate Conception—Immaculate meaning perfectly clean and pure.

That ideal of virginity and purity was a cornerstone of Ancient Egyptian traditions. Such was depicted as Ancient Egyptian women wearing a vulture headdress.

The choice of the vulture for this particular feminine role is because:

1. The vulture is supposed to be particularly zealous in caring for its young.
2. There is no physical sexual contact between male and female vultures. The female vulture impregnates herself by exposing herself to receive the male seeds carried by the winds. The vulture is therefore a symbol of *virgin birth*.

4.4 THE VIRGIN MOTHER OF 'GOD'

Isis' conception of Horus by no living man is the oldest documented version of immaculate conception. She was always revered as **the Virgin Mother**.

Several of her attributes in the Ancient Egyptian texts describe Isis as:

> *"The mother of god.*
> *Whose son is the lord of the earth"*

Isis' role in the Egyptian Model Story and the story of the Virgin Mary are strikingly similar, for both were able to conceive without male impregnation and, as such, Isis was revered as the Virgin Mother.

The 6th century BCE statue of Isis and her son, now in the Turin Museum, inspired the 15th century painter Masaccio in his presentation of *The Virgin and Child*. This image was plentiful in the Ancient Egyptian artifacts. We can easily find one or several such statues in museums throughout the world.

4.5 MARY ISIS AND CHILD REFUGE INTO EGYPT

In the Egyptian allegory of Isis, the story goes that when the Evil One—Seth—heard about the new child Horus, Seth went to kill the newborn.

Hearing that the evil tyrant Seth was coming, Isis was told to take him to a secluded spot in the marshes of the Nile Delta.

What happened to Isis is strikingly similar to the Bible

story in which Herod, upon hearing about the birth of the biblical Jesus, set out to destroy all the newborn males.

In the New Testament, the angel of the Lord says to Joseph:

"Arise and take the young child and his mother and flee into Egypt."

4.6 THE DIVINE SACRIFICE

In Ancient Egypt, the Mother deity, Isis, had a son who, in the form of a bull, was sacrificed annually in order to assure the cycle of the seasons and the continuity of Nature.

As per present practices, ancient writers asserted that it was the mother who was chosen to produce a calf with particular qualities—he was *The Bull of His Mother*, so to speak. Herodotus, in describing him, says:

"Apis, also called Epaphus, is a young bull, whose mother can have no other offspring, and who is reported by the Egyptians to conceive from lightning sent from heaven, and thus to produce the bull-god Apis".

The religious connotations of this sacrifice are an echo of a sacrifice in the sacrament, where we are reminded of Christ's death so that mankind might be saved. In essence, this is a genuine religious drama in which, as in the Catholic Mass, a god is worshiped and sacrificed.

One of the most important rituals in the Egyptian annual festivals since ancient times is the ritual sacrifice of the bull, which represents the renewal of the cosmic forces through the death and resurrection of the bull deity.

CHAPTER 5 : THE NUMEROLOGY OF ISIS & OSIRIS

5.1 THE PRIMARY NUMBERS OF ISIS AND OSIRIS (2 & 3)

In the animated world of Ancient Egypt, numbers did not simply designate quantities but instead were considered to be concrete definitions of energetic formative principles of nature. The Egyptians called these energetic principles neteru (gods, goddesses).

For Egyptians, numbers were not just odd and even—they were male and female. Every part of the universe was/is a male or a female.

Egyptians manifested their knowledge of number mysticism in all aspects of their lives. The evidence that Egypt possessed this knowledge is commanding.

The two primary numbers in the universe are those of Isis and Osiris—being the numbers 2 and 3 – such as that was described in the description of the 3:4:5 triangle by Plutarch in *Moralia Vol. V*:

> *"The upright, therefore, may be likened to the male, the base to the female, and the hypotenuse to the child of*

> *both, and so Osiris may be regarded as the origin, Isis as the recipient, and Horus as perfected result.*
>
> *Three is the first perfect odd number: four is a square whose side is the even number two; but five is in some ways like to its father, and in some ways like to its mother, being made up of three and two. And panta [all] is a derivative of pente [five], and they speak of counting as "numbering by fives Five makes a square of itself."*

The vitality and the interactions between these numbers show how they are male and female, active and passive, vertical and horizontal, etc.

For the Egyptians, one was not a number, but the essence of the underlying principle of number; all other numbers being made of it.

Isis is the number 2 [the square of 2 is 4]—female—even—base, etc.

Osiris is the number 3—male—odd—upright, etc.

Horus is number 5, the combined result [offspring] of the numbers 2 and 3.

Two symbolizes the power of multiplicity—the female, mutable receptacle – while Three symbolizes the male. This was the music of the spheres—the universal harmonies played out between these two primal male and female universal symbols of Isis and Osiris whose heavenly marriage produced the child Horus (number 5).

All phenomena, without exception, are polar in nature

and treble in principle. Therefore, five is the key to understanding the manifested universe, which Plutarch explained in the Egyptian context:

"...And panta (all) is a derivative of pente (five)..."

5.2 THE PRIMARY GENERATING NUMBERS OF SHAPES AND FORMS

From the roots of Two, Three, and Five, all harmonic proportions and relationships can be derived. The interplay of these proportions and relations commands the forms of all matter, organic and inorganic, and all processes and sequences of growth.

The role of a root in a plant is the same exact role/function as that of the root in geometry. The root of a plant assimilates, generates, and transforms energies to the rest of the plant.

Likewise, the geometric root is an archetypal expression of the assimilative, generating, transformative function and process; whereas fixed, whole numbers are the structures that emerge to build upon these principles of process.

Design that is based on root rectangles is called generative dynamic design, which the ancient Egyptians practiced for at least 4,500 years. The three sacred roots of Two, Three, and Five are all that are necessary for the formation of the five cosmic solids [tetrahedron, hexahedron, octahedron, icosahedron and dodecahedron] which are the basis for all volumetric forms, where all edges and all interior angles are equal.

The sequence of the numerical creation of Isis, followed by Osiris, followed by Horus, is 2, 3, 5, ...

It is a progressive series, where you start with the two primary numbers in the Ancient Egyptian system – i.e. 2 and 3. Then you add their total to the preceding number, and on and on—any figure is the sum of the two preceding ones. The series would therefore be:

2
3
5 (3+2)
8 (5+3)
13 (8+5)
21 (13+8)
34 (21+13)
55 (34+21)
89, 144, 233, 377, 610 ...

The Summation Series is reflected throughout nature. The number of seeds in a sunflower, the petals of any flower, the arrangement of pine cones, the growth of a nautilus shell, etc.—all follow the same pattern of these series.

[See more information about this Summation series and its use in Ancient Egypt for at least 4,500 years in *The Ancient Egyptian Metaphysical Architecture* or its older edition, being *Egyptian Harmony: The Visual Music;* both by Moustafa Gadalla.]

5.3 THE MUSICAL DYNAMO

For the Egyptians, Isis and Osiris regulated the music of the spheres. The universal harmonies are played out between these two primal male and female universal symbols of Isis and Osiris, whose heavenly marriage produced a son, Horus.

Musically, the ratio/relationship of 2:3 on the vibrating string and on the keyboard determines the vibration of the Perfect Fifth, reaching through five intervals.

On a monochord, the sound of the natural Fifth is produced when the string is held down at a point that divides the string into a 2:3.

The interval of the Fifth affords the strongest possible harmony between any two different tones. It is the first harmonic interval to which all other harmonic intervals relate.

Plutarch stated the importance of the Fifth for the Egyptians in his *Moralia, Vol. V*:

> ***And panta (all) is a derivative of pente (five), and they [the Egyptians] speak of counting as "numbering by fives".***

The Ancient Egyptians counted "by fives", and the strongest and most natural progression from one harmony to another is the result of such development.

All musical scales are generated through the progression of the Fifth. The form/relation of this first consonance is the first Fifth established by the heavenly marriage of Isis and Osiris. They, in turn, became a model to form, by a succession of similar relations, in a geometric progression.

Harmonic progression along the cycle of Perfect Fifths is the most natural, and a succession of harmonies not in this relation has the character of a delay or suspension of this natural progression. The whole musical system flows from only one given Fifth, which naturally must be in the same proportion as the first. There was no tampering with this proportion and no substitution for another one.

[More detailed information is found in *The Enduring Ancient Egyptian Musical System* or its earlier edition, *Egyptian Rhythm*, both by Moustafa Gadalla.]

5.4 THE BINARY AND TERNARY UNIVERSAL RHYTHM

The numbers 2 and 3 are related to the natural breathing rhythm. When a person is in a quiet sleep, the time between expiration and inhalation is twice as long as that between inhalation and exhalation. It is the idea behind all musical forms. The in-and-out and the alternation of tension and relaxation governs all further manifestations.

Also, practically all rhythmic organization is based on one of two general schemes: the binary (strong, alternating with a weak beat), or ternary (strong, followed by two weak beats). One or the other of these types underlies the rhythmic framework of every composition. The underlying binary or ternary rhythm is known as the fundamental rhythm.

Subdivisions of these beats that appear within the general framework are called the subsidiary rhythm. [See more details in *The Enduring Ancient Egyptian Musical System* by Moustafa Gadalla.]

CHAPTER 6 : ISIS' MULTITUDE OF ATTRIBUTES

ISIS OF THE 10,000 NAMES/ATTRIBUTES

The divine female principle of Isis manifests itself into numerous feminine-related attributes, and therefore the ancient Egyptians called her Isis of the 10,000 names (meaning attributes). This was affirmed by Plutarch, where he writes in his *Moralia Vol. V:*

> *"... since, because of the force of Reason. Isis turns herself to this thing or that and is receptive of all manner of shapes and forms".*

Since Isis represents the universal female principle, she is manifested into numerous forms. It is therefore that she is described in the Ancient Egyptian texts as:

> *"Isis of the 10,000 names [meaning attributes]"*

> *"She of many names."*

Here we present several various manifestations of the female principle in her various attributes, such as:

1- Maat

2- Seshat
3- Net [Neith]
4- Nut—Firmament
5- Nephthys
6- Satet
7- Ta-urt
8- Mut
9- Sekh-mut—The Den Mother
10- Bast—The Docile Cat
11- Qadesh
12- Heqet
13- Serket
14- Anat
15- Hathor—Venus—Merit—Astarte

>>> **It should be noted that the digital edition of this book as published in PDF and E-book formats has a substantial number of photographs that compliment the text materials throughout this chapter.**

6.1 MAAT

Maat is one of the manifestations of the female principle in the universe. Isis in her attribute as Maat represents the model for cosmic harmony, order, balance, and equilibrium.

Ma-at is usually portrayed as a woman wearing a headdress with an ostrich plume attached.

The concept of Ma-at has permeated all Egyptian writings, from the earliest times and throughout Egyptian history. It is the concept by which not only humankind but also all the powers in the universe are governed. Maat signifies harmony, balance, and equilibrium between all the cosmic forces of the universe.

Ma-at is not easily translated or defined by one word. Basically, we might say that it means that which, of right, should be; that which is according to the proper order and harmony of the cosmos and of neteru (gods, goddesses) and men who are part of it.

In human terms, Ma-at represents the right thing to do. Ma-at could be favorably compared with the Eastern concept of *karma* and the Western concept of *common sense*.

Ma-at represents the abstract concept of order, justice, truth, righteousness, and what is right, in all their purest forms. Ma-at is the ideal of balance: of things working as they should. Without Maat, chaos reigns unchecked, and the ability to create order is forever lost. That is to say, Ma-at is order in its most abstract level—that which causes everything to exist and to continue to exist.

The application of the Ma-at principle extends to every aspect of Egyptian life. As the model for cosmic harmony, order, balance, and equilibrium, Ma-at is associated with many functions. We will briefly mention a few such applications:

A. Maat's Cosmic Role in

i- The pre-creation planning
ii- The dual nature of creation
iii- The orderly plan of creation

B. Maat and the Earthly Voyage

i- Daily Activities and Temple Rituals
ii- The Harmonic Laws of Music
iii- Societal Order
iv- The Spiritual Path
v- Justice for All—On Earth and After Earth

6.1.A. Maat's Cosmic Role

Ma-at is the netert (goddess) that represents the principle of cosmic order; the concept by which not only men, but also the neteru (gods) themselves, were governed; and without which the neteru (gods) are functionless.

We will briefly mention a few such applications:

Maat's role in:

i- the pre creation planning
ii- the dual nature of creation
iii- the orderly process of creation

i- Maat in the Pre-Creation Planning

For the deeply religious people of Egypt, the creation of the universe was not a physical event (Big Bang) that just happened. The explosion (Big Bang) that led to the creation of the universe was an orderly and pre-planned event—unlike all other explosions that exhibit a random and disordered form.

So, we read in the *Book of Knowing the Creations of Re and Overcoming Apep (Apophis)*, known as the *Bremner-Rhind Papyrus*:

> **"I had not yet found a place upon which I could stand. I conceived the Divine Plan of Law or Order (Maa) to make all forms. I was alone . . ."**

All Egyptian texts emphasize again and again that the concept and details of creation was pre-planned according to an orderly form before the actual creation occurred.

ii- The Dual Nature of Creation—Maati

The world as we know it is held together by a law that is based on the balanced dual nature of all things (wholes, units). Each pair represents a different aspect of the same fundamental principle of polarity. And each aspect partakes of the nature of unity and duality.

The Egyptians perceived the universe in terms of a dualism between Ma-at—Truth and Order—and disorder. The creation of the cosmos was summoned out of undifferentiated chaos by distinguishing the two and by giving voice to the ultimate ideal of Truth. Ma-at, as shown below, is usually portrayed in the double form—Maati.

iii- The Orderly Process of Creation

The Ancient Egyptian papyrus known as the Bremner-Rhind Papyrus tells us that before the creation took place, the master of the universe conceived the Divine Plan of Law or Order to make all forms:

> *"I conceived in my own heart; there came into being a vast number of forms of divine beings as the forms of offsprings and the forms of their offsprings."*

In the simplest terms, the Egyptian text tells us that the created world is basically a hierarchy of energies. This hierarchy is interrelated, and each level is sustained by the level below it. This hierarchy of energies is set neatly into a vast matrix of deeply interfaced natural laws represented in the form of *'offsprings and the forms of their offsprings.'*

6.1.B. Maat and the Earthly Voyage

    i- Daily Activities and Temple Rituals
    ii- The Harmonic Laws of Music
    iii- Societal Order

iv- The Spiritual Path
v- Justice for All—On Earth and After Earth

i- Daily Activities and Temple Rituals

As the model for cosmic harmony, order, balance, and equilibrium, Ma-at is associated with many functions. All the activities of the Egyptian life, including building temples, were devoted to the maintenance of Ma-at.

The temple's rituals were based upon and coordinated with the movements of the heavens which were, in turn, manifestations of the divine cosmic law.

ii- Ma-at governs the harmonic laws of music.

As the model for cosmic harmony, order, balance, and equilibrium, Ma-at is associated with many functions, such as the harmonic laws of music.

Music is all about balance. Maintaining Ma-at is to maintain harmony, balance, and equilibrium in everything—including music. Ma-at's representations are found as "decoration" on many Egyptian instruments.

The experts in music were called musicians/priests of Ma-at and teaching instruments were/are called *Mizan*—meaning balance/scale.

Harmony is characterized by an unmistakable sense of 'equilibrium'. Equilibrium is a state in which positive and negative forces are balanced. Ma-at is usually depicted next to a balanced scale.

The world as we know it is held together by a law that is based on the balanced dual nature of all things (wholes, units). Balance occurs between complementary opposites. Ma-at is usually depicted next to the typical Ancient Egyptian scale with two unequal weights, therefore requiring balancing by the plumb bob. The plumb bob determines the vertical and governs the equilibrium of the scales. Scenes of weighing show that it is necessary to still the plumb line, because otherwise it would continue to oscillate.

The Ancient Egyptian term for oscillation, intoxication, and plumb bob is *tkh*.

The plumb bob, *tkh*, is very often modeled in the form of the heart, or *ib, the Dancer*. The heartbeat provides us with a convenient measure of time.

iii- Maat as the Societal Order

Ma-at is related to societal orderly relationship and harmony.

In order to achieve perfect universal harmony, the social structure must mirror the same orderly hierarchy of the created universe.

Human survival and success require that the same orderly structure be maintained. As above so below is the only way to achieve order and harmony.

The matriarchal system, as the social manifestation of planetary laws, was the basis of the social organization in Ancient Egypt, as explained earlier in Chapter 3 of this book.

iv- Maat as the Spiritual Path

As the model for cosmic harmony, order, balance, and equilibrium, Ma-at represents the spiritual path that each individual must follow.

Ma-at is maintained in the world by the correct actions and personal piety of its adherents. The ultimate objective of the earthly man is to develop his/her consciousness to the utmost perfection. This means that he/she becomes harmoniously tuned with nature.

Ma-at represents the spiritual path that each individual must follow. The Egyptian model recognizes the uniqueness of each individual, and as such, recognizes that paths to the divine are as numerous as the number of seekers. The ways to the divine are like streams—they all go to one source.

The Ancient Egyptians implemented their beliefs in individuality in all their texts. There were never two identical transformational (funerary) or medical (so-called "magical") texts for any two individuals. One must live his or her own life, and each one of us must go his or her own way, guided by Ma-at.

The Ancient Egyptian religion is not a matter of creed and dogma, but rather of a personal charter. Each one of us is an individual. One must live his/her own life, and each one of us must go his/her own way, guided by Maat.

Ma-at, The Way, encompasses the virtues, goals, and duties that define acceptable, if not ideal, social interactions and personal behavior. Ma-at is maintained in the world by the correct actions and personal piety of its adherents.

The Ancient Egyptian wisdom has always laid great emphasis on the cultivation of ethical behavior and service to society. The constant theme of Egyptian wisdom literature was the 'acting out' of Truth—*MaaKheru*—on Earth. The expected conduct and the ideas of responsibility and retribution were expressed in several literary compositions that are usually called 'wisdom texts'.

There were additional practical wisdom texts of systematic instructions, composed of maxims and precepts.

[For more information about the spiritual path, read *Egyptian Mystics: Seekers of the Way* by Moustafa Gadalla.]

v- Maat as Lady Justice—Both on Earth and After Earth

As the model for cosmic harmony, order, balance, and equilibrium, Ma-at is associated with many functions, such as the administration of justice, both on Earth and after Earth.

Ma-at is the Egyptian lady of justice. Our symbol of modern-day justice is a blindfolded lady, carrying a scale. Such symbolism is derived from Ma-at—the ancient Egyptian's symbol of justice—a blindfolded lady. Ma-at is depicted in her role as lady of justice, **"*having her eyes closed*"** to ensure equal justice for all.

Ma-at is often shown in a double form, representing the two opposing sides of a litigation, because the scale of justice cannot balance without the equality of opposing forces.

Judgment Day is held in what the Egyptians called *Hall of Two Maati*.

The Egyptian lady of justice is portrayed as a woman with her symbol, the ostrich feather mounted on her head, and holding the emblem of truth to emphasize the main concept of justice—search for the truth. The Maat symbol is the feather of truth/ostrich used in the scale of justice.

As attested to by Diodorus, all judges of high rank in Ancient Egypt were described as priests of Ma-at, and the chief justice wore a little figure of Ma-at around his neck as a badge of office.

The ultimate objective of the earthly man is to develop his/her consciousness to the utmost perfection. This means that he/she becomes harmoniously tuned with nature. This was symbolized in some Egyptian tombs by the deceased soul reciting the 42 Negative Confessions, on the Judgment Day, before 42 jurors/neteru. The successful person was declared to be Sound, by the Grand Jury, as *Maa Kheru*—True of Voice.

The soul of the deceased is led to the Hall of Judgment of the Double-Ma-at. She is double because the scale balances only when there is an equality of opposing forces. Ma-at's symbol is the ostrich feather, representing judgment or truth. Her feather is customarily mounted on the scales.

The heart, as a metaphor for conscience, is weighed against the feather of truth to determine the fate of the deceased.

[For more detailed information on the subject of life after Earth, read *Egyptian Cosmology: The Animated Universe* by Moustafa Gadalla.]

6.2 SESHAT

Seshat is another one of the manifestations of Isis' role as the Divine Intellect. Seshat represents the organizational capacity of keeping records—knowledge, information, etc. [shown below at the far left of the middle register].

Seshat is depicted carrying the reed pen and palette, and records deeds in eternity/space (i.e. memory).

Seshat (or Sefekht, meaning seven) is usually depicted wearing the panther skin, denoting primordial power, with a seven-petaled flower on her head.

Seshat is referred to as: *The Enumerator, Lady of Writing(s), Scribe, Head of the House of the Divine Books (Archives), Lady of Builders*, etc.

She is commonly shown in scenes depicting the laying of the foundation of a new temple. In this regard, she is described as the *Lady of Builders.*

Seshat is closely associated with Thoth, and is considered to be his female counterpart.

As the keeper of records, Seshat is usually depicted recording at scenes of the Tree of Life.

6.3 NET [NEITH]

Net [Neith] is another example of the manifestations of

Isis' role as the Divine Intellect by setting harmonic patterns.

In such a role, she is recognized as Net or Neith, representing the divine process of setting harmonic patterns, as symbolized by the act of weaving.

A few of the 10,000 attributes of Isis call her:

> **Lady of the shuttle.**
> **Isis... Weaver and Fuller.**

Net [Neith] is portrayed as a woman carrying two crossed arrows. She wears a weaving shuttle upon her head. Weaving is accomplished by the crossing of nerves and fibers. These two arrows represent the two directions of crossing.

Net [Neith] represents the ability to establish a pattern by creating a netted fabric by weaving, or determining the pattern of behavior of someone or something.

Not coincidentally, Net [Neith] is one of the four canopic

jar patrons and is the protector of the stomach, which is the seat of process and digestion—both physically and metaphysically.

6.4 NUT—FIRMAMENT

In her role as the firmament, Isis is recognized as **Nut**.

Nut is associated with many related functions, such as:

> A. The Firmament of Heaven
>
> B. Nut and Geb—The Celestial Sphere
>
> C. Nut The Heavenly Astronomical Starry Sky, as she relates to:
>
>> – sun/solar and moon/lunar principles
>> – zodiac cycle
>
> D. Nut the Spirit of the Sky; as being present in:
>
>> – coffins and coffin lids
>> – Tomb chambers
>> – Tree of life Nourishment and Rebirth

6.4.A. The Firmament of Heaven

The firmament as heaven is described in ancient Egypt as the sky, viewed poetically as a solid arch or vault. The ancient Egyptian texts describe Isis as:

Queen of heaven
Queen of the Firmament.

In her role as the firmament, Isis is recognized as Nut.

Nut is depicted in several forms; but often as a naked woman arched over the heavens, in the act of swallowing the evening sun and giving birth to the morning sun. The new sun is often shown in its form of the scarab beetle. Nut represents the sky as matrix of all—the cosmic source of nourishment.

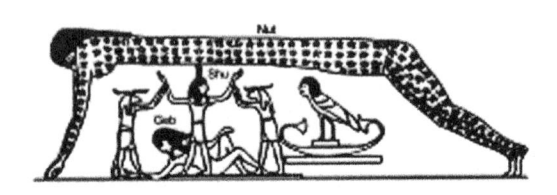

6.4.B. Nut and Geb—The Celestial Sphere

Duality is the natural manifestation of creation. In this light, Nut as a female principle has a mirror image, counter, male partner. Nut's male counterpart is Geb. Geb represents the material/physical aspects of the universe.

Geb is depicted as a man bearing a goose upon his head. This representation is the source of the worldwide notion about the goose that laid the golden egg from which the world was hatched.

In scientific terms, the egg is the celestial sphere—the universal bubble that contains all creation.

In this celestial sphere, Geb represents the phenomenal or physical world and Nut represents the noumenal or metaphysical world.

6.4.C. Nut The Heavenly Astronomical Starry Sky

Nut is depicted as a star-studded woman arched over the heavens.

Strikingly, in the first book of Genesis, we read:

> *"And God said, Let there be lights in the firmament of the heaven".*

Genesis I, 14 reads:

> *"14: And God said, Let there be lights in the firmament of the heaven to divide the day from the night; and let them be for signs, and for seasons, and for days, and years:"*

The implications here are that the changes observed in the sky are correlated to changes on earth—such as the seasonal cycles.

The cyclical nature of the universe—in whole or in part—is a constant and consistent theme in the Ancient Egyptian texts.

Nut is depicted as arched over the heavens in the act of swallowing the evening sun and giving birth to the morning sun. The new sun is often shown in the form of scarab beetle—a new beginning; a rebirth.

One of Isis' 10,000 attributes describe her as:

> *The Queen of the Dekan stars.*

Genesis I, 16-17 reads:

> *16: And God made two great lights; the greater light to rule the day, and the lesser light to rule the night: he made the stars also.*
>
> *17: And God set them in the firmament of the heaven to give light upon the earth,*

Genesis I, 16, refers to the creation of the *"greater light"* of the day and the *"lesser light"* of the night. The reference is clearly made to the sun and the moon.

In the Egyptian model, Isis represents the sun and Osiris represents the moon. To the Egyptians, the sun and moon provide more than light during the day and night times. Here is how significant are they to creation and maintaining the universe, as foretold by Diodorus of Sicily in his *Book I*, [11. 5-6]:

> *These two neteru (gods)—Isis and Osiris —they hold, regulate the entire universe, giving both nourishment and increase to all things...*

Then Diodorus explains the Ancient Egyptian reasoning for the significance of the sun and moon on the universal existence, as follows:

> *Moreover, practically all the physical matter which is essential to the generation of all things is furnished by these two neteru (gods), Isis and Osiris, symbolized as the sun and the moon. The sun contributing the fiery element and the spirit, the moon the wet and the dry, and both together the air; and it is through these elements that all things are engendered and nourished.*
>
> *And so it is out of the sun and moon that the whole*

> *physical body of the universe is made complete; and as for the five parts just named of these bodies-the spirit, the fire, the dry, as well as the wet, and, lastly, the air- just as in the case of a man we enumerate head and hands and feet and the other parts, so in the same way the body of the universe is composed in its entirety of these parts.*

Reference to the creation of the stars is given at the end of Genesis I, 16:

> *16: And God made two great lights; the greater light to rule the day, and the lesser light to rule the night: he made the stars also.*
> *17: And God set them in the firmament of the heaven to give light upon the earth*

To the Ancient Egyptians, the stars have much more significance than to just *"give light upon the earth."*

The Egyptian Nut is always associated with the constellations in the sky. Most noticeable are the zodiac signs that were found in Egyptian tombs and temples many centuries before the Greek era.

[More details about the subject of astronomy and zodiac are detailed in *Ancient Egyptian Culture Revealed* by Moustafa Gadalla.]

6.4.D. Nut the Spirit of the Sky

Nut as the Spirit of the Sky is prominently depicted in the resting places of the Ancient Egyptians, in tomb chambers, coffins, and coffin lids.

As the nourishing mother spirit of heaven, Nut springs out from the tree of life to offer the souls of the deceased an everlasting metaphysical nourishment.

6.5 NEPHTHYS—ISIS' TWIN SISTER

Nephthys as the universal dual aspect of Isis was addressed in Chapter 2 of this book. Here we will provide more information about Nephthys by herself.

Nephthys' Egyptian name is **Nebt-Het** which means golden/noblest/mistress (**Nebt**) *of the place/house* (**Het**).

Nephthys is portrayed as a woman wearing upon her head the symbols that are read as her name.

Nephthys is one of the four canopic jar patrons, protecting the lungs.

Isis protects the liver.

Serket protects the intestines.

Net (Neith) protects the stomach.

6.6 SATET

Satet (Satis) is one of Isis' attributes as 'Mother Time'. In such a role, Satet (Satis) is associated with Sabt (Sirius/Sothis)' the star of Isis that ushered in the beginning of the Ancient Egyptian New Sothic Year and the Nile inundation season.

Satis is depicted as a woman wearing the white crown with antelope horns.

In several of her attributes, Isis is described in Ancient Egyptian texts as:

> **Sothis, who openeth the New Year.**
> **The lady of the beginning of the year.**

[For more about astronomy in Ancient Egypt, read *Ancient Egyptian Culture Revealed* by Moustafa Gadalla.]

6.7 TA-URT

Isis, in her role as the Divine Pregnant Mother, is recognized as Ta-urt.

Ta-urt or Thoueri is also known under the names Apt and Sheput.

Her common titles are *"mistress of the neteru* (gods, goddesses)*"* and *"bearer of the neteru* (gods, goddesses)*"*. Taurt is thus the patroness of children and maternity in the earthly realm. She represents the Midwife par excellence—both physically and metaphysically.

Ta-urt is found at the beginning of each cycle, such as the zodiac cycle, as depicted in numerous places prior to the Greek era.

Ta-urt is portrayed as an upright hippopotamus with pendulous breasts, lion's paws, and a crocodile's tail.

Ta-urt as Apt/Opt—Ta-urt is also referred to as Apet/Opet.

In her form of Ipet/Opet/Apet, Ta-urt plays a crucial role in the largest temple in Egypt – namely the Karnak Temple complex at Ta-**Apet** (Thebes/Luxor).

The Ancient Egyptian name for the Karnak temple itself is **Apet**-sut, which means *Enumerator of the Places*. The design and enumeration in this temple are consistent with the creation and growth numerical codes. [The principles and applications of such numerical and geometrical codes can be found in the book *The Ancient Egyptian Metaphysical Architecture* or its older edition, *Egyptian Harmony: The Visual Music;* both by Moustafa Gadalla.]

One of the most prominent festivals in Luxor since ancient times is the **Apet** Festival.

The Ancient Egyptian name for Luxor is **Ta-Apet,** and one needs say no more.

6.8 MUT

The Ancient Egyptian texts refer to Isis, in her role as the divine mother, as being:

> ***The mother of neter*** (god)—being Horus.

Mut, as she is referred to in such a role, represents the principle of motherhood in its purest abstract form.

The term Mut is connected linguistically with the many similar-sounding words for mother, found in many languages.

Mut is usually depicted as a woman with the body of the vulture so artfully formed to her own head that it passes for a headdress.

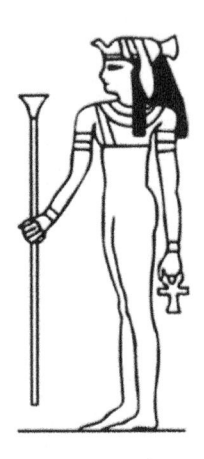

The reasons for choosing the vulture for this particular feminine role are:

1. The vulture is supposed to be particularly zealous in caring for its young.
2. The female vulture gets impregnated by exposing herself to the male sperm carried by the winds, and not through direct contact with males. The vulture is, therefore, a symbol of virgin birth (in other words, purity). Purity of the body and soul is a prerequisite to advancing into higher realms.

Mut is found in many places and in many forms, such as with Sekhmet, Hathor, Nut, and with Bast; among many others.

6.9 SEKH-MUT—THE DEN MOTHER

Isis, in her role as the 'Den Mother', is recognized as Sekhmet or Sekhmut. This is actually two words: Sekh and Mut—meaning 'Elder' or the 'Den Mother'.

As the Den Mother, Sekh-Mut is portrayed, in Egyptian representations, as a lioness. Sekhmet statues are usually made of igneous rocks such as basalt or granite, emphasizing her passionate, fiery nature.

Sekh-Mut represents the fiery aspect of creative power.

In the Litany of Re, Re is described (in one of his 75 forms/attributes) as **The One of the Cat** and as **The Great Cat**.

As the Divine Den Mother, Sekh-Mut is usually portrayed as a woman with exposed breasts and the head of a lioness surmounted by the sun's disk, around which is a uraeus.

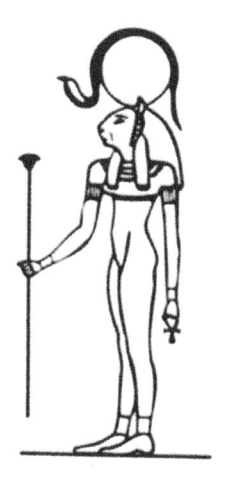

As the Divine Den mother, she projects:

a. an urge/passion/desire/will to create. To present her urge/passion/desire/will to create, Sekh-Mut is depicted with an ithyphallic male body.

b. Passionate, tender, loving care. Depictions show her supporting/encouraging others with tender, loving gestures.

c. Passionate, fearless protection of her creation. To show her passionate fearless protection of her creation, SekhMut statues are found at the entry point to temples—such as in Medinet Hapu in Luxor,

The lioness is the most fearless animal on earth. In our modern societies, the guts and spine are symbols of physical courage. This concept has Ancient Egyptian roots. In the *Papyrus of Ani* [pl.32 item 42], we read:

> ***my belly and my spine are Sekh-Mut***

Sekh-Mut is almost always depicted with Khonsu—she representing the female solar principle and he (Khonsu) representing the male lunar principle.

6.10 BAST—THE DOCILE CAT

Isis, in her role as the center of calmness, is the docile cat Bast or Bastet.

In the litany of Re, he is described as The One of the Cat and The Great Cat. The nine realms of the universe are manifested in the cat; for both the cat and the Grand Ennead (meaning the nine times unity) have the same ancient Egyptian term 'b.st'. This relationship has found its way into Western culture, where one says that *'**the cat has nine lives**'*.

Bast represents the gentle and docile aspect of the cat, as opposed to Sekh-Mut, the fiery lioness.

Bast is usually depicted as cat-headed.

Bast represents the total harmony within—the sense of internal happiness, contentment and peace.

Herodotus wrote about the annual festivities around the Bast temple of Tell Basta (Bubastis), just outside Zagazig, in the Nile Delta.

The annual festivities of this ancient city attracted more than 700,000 people. Herodotus described their joy during the Bast celebrations.

6.11 QADESH

Here, we study Isis in her role as the symbol for the legal heiress, as being Qadesh.

Qadesh represents legitimacy.

Qadesh means 'holy' or 'sacred' in Ancient Egyptian.

Qadesh is often represented as a young woman standing on a lion's back, signifying the matrilineal/matriarchal principle.

Qadesh is ordained and described in Ancient Egyptian texts as the Beloved of Ptah.

Qadesh is also associated with Hathor in her role as Astrarte, Patroness of Travelers.

It is therefore that we find that Qadesh's depiction from Memphis more than 4,000 years ago is also found in Yemen at the southern end of the Red Sea, in later times. This shows the vigorous sea trading that took place during Ancient Egyptian times, thousands of years ago.

6.12 HEQET

Isis, in her role as symbol of fertility, is recognized as Heqet.

Heqet represents conception and procreation; i.e. she is the source of life; and as such, she is always depicted near divine conception scenes in Egyptian monuments.

Heqet is depicted as a frog-headed woman, or as a frog.

Heqet is associated with Khnum and the annual inundation. Frogs always appeared in large numbers just before the annual flooding of the Nile. Frog amulets were/are popular for fertility because of the frog's procreative nature.

6.13 SERKET

Isis, in her role as a protector, is recognized as Serket.

Serket (Selkis) represents the zealous protection aspect of motherhood.

Serket (Selkis) is identified with the scorpion, which is famous for its protection of its young.

Serket (Selkis), as an aspect of Isis, represents the protection and nurturing of young children.

Serket (Selkis) is usually depicted as a woman with a scorpion on her head – or sometimes as a scorpion with a woman's head.

Serket (Selkis) is one of the patrons of the four canopic jars, protecting the intestines.

6.14 ANAT

Isis, in her role as a guardian, is recognized as Anat. A good guard is always ready to deter any outside threat. Therefore, Anat is represented as a woman holding a shield and an axe.

Anat is the guardian (not a "warrior goddess") of Egypt's eastern frontier at Tanis; and as such, Anat represents wilderness—an aspect of Seth. Anat is also associated with the lioness Sekh-Met, the fearless one.

6.15 HATHOR—VENUS

Isis, in her role as the Nourisher, is recognized as Hathor.

Hathor is actually two words, Het-hor, which is commonly translated as *"house of of Horus"*.

The first part—**Het**, translated as "house", has a bigger meaning than a simple house. It actually means *the womb as a Matrix* within which something originates, takes form, and develops into full maturity.

The womb provides nourishment and protection. As such, Hethor provides both nourishment and protection. Horus represents the realized divine principle, and Horus is recognized by various names/attributes as he develops from infancy to maturity within the cosmic womb.

Hathor represents the matrix of the metaphysical spiritual principle, providing spiritual nourishment, healing, joy, lovemaking, music, and cheerfulness.

The Ancient Egyptian texts describe Isis of the 10,000 Names in her role of Het-heru as:

> **The Cow Heru-sekha, who brings forth all things.**
> **Who nourished the child Horus with her milk.**

Lady of joy and gladness.

Lady of Love

As the model for cosmic nourishment of all kinds, Hathor is associated with several related functions. We will briefly mention a few such applications:

    A. Lady Love—Venus
    B. The Cosmic Nourisher
    C. The Heavenly Seven Maidens /7 Heavenly Realms
    D. The Healer
    E. Her Tree of Life
    F. The Ultimate Shrine—House of Horus/Re-horakhti
    G. Travelers Escort—Astarte

6.15.A. Lady Love—Venus

The dictionary tells us that the origin of the name (or word) Venus is WENOS. Wenos or Wanas is actually an Egyptian word meaning 'animated companionship', 'genial', 'sociable', 'cheerful', and 'pleasurable'.

The noun form of we-nos is A-nesa [Aa-NES-sa], meaning 'maiden', with all that it implies.

The Egyptian Venus, in her all-encompassing name of Hathor, represents the matrix of the metaphysical spiritual principle, providing spiritual nourishment, healing, joy, lovemaking, music, and cheerfulness.

6.15.B. The Cosmic Nourisher—Madonna

As the great provider of spiritual nourishment, Hathor is often depicted as a cow-headed woman; or entirely in human form, but with cow ears. The cow is the ideal representation for nourishment of all kinds and, as such, is the ideal symbol for Hathor.

She wears a variety of headdresses; most commonly a pair of horns enclosing the solar disk.

On the cosmic level, Hathor is depicted in full cow form to symbolize the cosmic concept/attribute of nourishment.

We will highlight, here, a few cow forms of Hathor:

– First, Hathor as the Celestial Cow **Mehet-Uret,** with her body spangled with stars.

Mehet-Uret (Mehurt, Methyer) represents the primeval

water; i.e. the watery abyss of heaven. Water is the source of life and sustenance.

Sometimes the king, as symbol for Horus, is shown taking milk from her udder.

Ancient Egyptian texts describe Isis of the 10,000 Names in her role of Hathor as:

> *The Cow Heru-sekha, who brings forth all things.*
> *Who nourished the child Horus with her milk.*

The Celestial cow are is depicted in seven cows. Hathor is associated with the number seven and was referred to as The Seven Hathors.

– **Hesat** is a form of Hathor, whose function it is to feed the youngsters.

Hesat represents the metaphysical nourishment (love, caring, singing, etc.) necessary for the growth and well-being of the children.

Breast feeding depictions represent both the physical as well as the meta-physical—spiritual nourishment. The most profound depiction is that of Isis in her form of Hathor, breast feeding Horus.

The Ancient Egyptian texts describe Isis of the 10,000 Names in her role of Hathor as:

Who nourished the child Horus with her milk.

This powerful representation served as the icon for The Madonna and Child. The Egyptian Madonna and her child are found in Egyptian works since at least the Old Kingdom era—5,000 years ago—as shown here in Saqqara, from this remote era.

Depictions in Egyptian temples of the breast feeding of young and older adults—by Hathor – represent spiritual nourishment; for we all need spiritual nourishment during his progression towards maturity.

Hathor, as the symbol of spiritual nourishment, also plays an important role in the transformational (funerary) texts, furnishing the spiritual nourishment required by the soul of the deceased.

6.15.C. The Heavenly Seven Maidens

Hathor is known as the *mistress of dance* and the *mistress of music*.

Hathor is associated with the seven natural tones of the diatonic scale and is/was called *"The Seven Hathors"*.

[More about music and dance is to be found in the book *The Enduring Ancient Egyptian Musical System* by Moustafa Gadalla.]

You may wonder—why seven?

The Egyptians believed that the universal energy matrix consists of 2 earthly realms and 7 heavenly realms.

Since Hathor represents the metaphysical aspects of the universe, she encompasses the seven heavenly realms.

Hathor is depicted wearing a sistrum—a musical rattle—on her head.

The text of the hymn of the "Song of the Seven Hathors" in the Temple of Dendera consists of seven stanzas; each of four lines.

The intimate relationship between music and the cosmos is clearly stated in one of the Seven Stanzas, as follows:

> *The sky and its stars make music to you.*
> *The sun and the moon praise you.*
> *The neteru* (gods, goddesses) *exalt you.*
> *The neteru* (gods, goddesses)*sing to you.*

The musical aspect of Hathor is symbolized by **Merit**.

Merit is the cosmic conductor/maestro who manages the notes and flow of musical performances.

The hand of Merit is the universal symbol of action. Musically, the fingers control the sound emitted from musical instruments. How you place fingers determines the tones. Therefore, fingers are the most logical way to express, write, and instruct music.

As a consequence, a certain note took its name from the string plucked or deadened by this finger. As such, fingers have often been used to describe the technique of striking, among the expressions of instrumental playing.

In Egypt (Ancient and Baladi), this conventional "finger movement" mode has been all that is needed to identify the different modes.

6.15.D. Hathor, The Healer

Isis in the form of Hathor represents the cure-all; and as such, mankind is always seeking her aid.

She protects and cares for and nourishes all creations. She uses her power graciously and successfully for all those who seek aid.

The populace of Egypt looked upon Isis as a patroness whose solicitude extended over the entire range of human needs.

Diodorus of Sicily, in *Book One*, describes the female caring qualities of Isis in her form as Hathor:

> *"The Egyptians say that she was the discoverer of many health-giving drugs and was greatly versed in the SCIENCE OF HEALING.*
>
> *Consequently, now that she has attained immortality, she finds her greatest delight in the healing of mankind and gives aid in their sleep to those who CALL upon her plainly manifesting both her very presence and her beneficence towards men who ask for her help.*
>
> *In proof of this, they say that practically the entire inhabited world is their witness in that it eagerly contributes to the honors of Isis because she manifests herself in healings. For standing above the sick in their sleep she gives them aid for their diseases and works remarkable cures upon such as submit themselves to her and many who have been despaired of by their physicians because of the difficult nature of their malady are restored to health by her while numbers who have altogether lost the use of their eyes or of some other part of their body, whenever they turn to her for help, are restored to their previous condition".*

By far, the largest number of shrines throughout Egyptian history were and continue to be dedicated to Hathor. There is practically no locality (small or large) in Egypt that does not have a shrine for the *Saba Banat* (meaning Seven Het-Heru). Such shrines are visited weekly by most Baladi women of Egypt.

Hathor is present in practically all temples and tombs,

such as Luxor (Thebes), Heliopolis, Memphis, Dendera, Abu Simbel, the mining regions of Sinai, and countless places between these major centers. Hathor's most prominent center was/is at Dendera.

Hathor temples were often healing centers. Hathor represents healing (a function also associated with Sekhmet). One of Dendera's most important roles was as a healing center where all manner of therapies were practiced (just like a hospital in our modern sense, more or less; but with more emphasis on healing the body and soul using all means; and not limited to surgical procedures).

6.15.E. Her Tree of Life

Hathor represents the metaphysical connections between our earthly existence and past ancestors. As such, Hathor represents the family tree.

People throughout the world refer to each other's "family tree". In Egypt, this term is fully understood as the residence of departed ancestors. As such, people often write notes and attach them to the branches of the tree. The tree becomes the medium between the departed and the living.

Hathor, therefore, represents the (family) tree netert (goddess).

Regarding the significance of Hathor's tree, Plutarch, in *Moralia Vol. V* (378, 68 G), states:

> *"Of the plants in Egypt they say that the persea is especially consecrated to the goddess Hathor because its fruit resembles a heart and its leaf a tongue".*

Plutarch's statement is affirmed by numerous Ancient Egyptian depictions [as shown herein] of Hathor springing from the Tree of Life to provide spiritual nourishment.

The universal rule of cause and effect—symbolized by the functions of the heart and tongue—is found on the Egyptian Shabaka Stele (716-701 BCE), as follows:

> **"The Heart and the Tongue have power over all . . . the neteru** (gods, goddesses), **all men, all cattle, all creeping things, and all that lives. The Heart thinks all that it wishes, and the Tongue delivers all that it wishes".**

6.15.F. The Ultimate Shrine—House of Horus/Re-Horakhti

Let us go over what Hathor represents, one more time.

Hathor is commonly translated by Western Egyptologists as **"house of of Horus"**.

The first part, Het, (translated as "house") has a bigger meaning than a simple house. It actually means the womb as a Matrix within which something originates, takes form, and develops into full maturity.

Horus represents the realized divine principle, and Horus is recognized by various names/attributes as he develops from infancy to maturity within the cosmic womb.

The final destination is unification with the creator as Re. At this point, the realized soul becomes Re-Hor-akhti. It is therefore that Het-hor is called the Lady of the West, residence of Horus, as Re-Herachti.

The realized soul—represented as the falcon wearing the sun disc—will be enshrined within Hathor as the tree of life; the Ultimate Shrine.

6.15.G. Travelers Escort—Astarte

Hathor has a prominent presence beyond the land of Egypt. Let us pause here again to see how and why her role is significant beyond the land of Egypt.

We have shown that the name and function of Hathor represents the cosmic womb. As such, Hathor provides both nourishment and protection, as we have seen showing throughout this presentation.

Beyond earthly existence, Hathor plays an important role in the transformational texts, furnishing the spiritual nourishment and guidance required by the soul of the deceased as it travels across the cosmic sea.

On Earth, Hathor provides a divine escort to travelers across the seas. Consequently, Hathor (also known as Aserah) is the Egyptian patroness of travel and sailing; and as a result, she appears in this role more often outside of Egypt.

Read more about her reverence outside Egypt and in festivals throughout the Mediterranean Basin at the end of the next chapter of this book.

CHAPTER 7 : THE BELOVED IN ALL LANDS

7.1 THE SPREAD OF THE EGYPTIAN RELIGION

In this chapter, we will follow the spread of Isis' ideology in the Mediterranean Basin and beyond—worldwide.

Isis, in one of her 10,000 names, is called

'Beloved in all lands".

Isis of the 10,000 Names, as well as other Ancient Egyptian deities, were adopted throughout the Mediterranean Basin and beyond. For example, the bas-reliefs, coins, and other antiquities that have been found in Thessaly, Epirus, Megara, Corinth, Argos, Malta, and many other places, portray Ancient Egyptian deities. Because of her many names and forms, the Greeks equated her with a number of goddesses of their pantheon: Persephone, Ceres, and Athens, among them. Herodotus, in the *Histories*, Book 2 [2-8], wrote:

> *"The names of nearly all the gods came to Greece from Egypt."*

This makes sense once we recognize two points that:

a. From the earliest days of comparative philology, it was noticed that the sounds of related languages corresponded in apparently systematic ways. As an example of the phenomenon of sound shift, a person's name can still be recognized in vastly different sounds, such as Santiago/San Diego/San Jacob and Saint James. Jacob/Jack/Jaques/James are one and the same name, which exemplifies the phenomenon of sound shift, where a letter that cannot be pronounced by a group of people is substituted by another sound that is easy for that group of people to pronounce.

b. It should be noted that what we commonly consider to be the *names* of deities are actually the "attributes" of such deities. The *real names* of the deities were kept secret. The real name was/is imbued with magical powers and properties. To know and pronounce the real name of a deity is to exercise power over it. To guard the cosmic power of the deity, the Ancient Egyptians (and later, others throughout the Mediterranean Basin and beyond) often used "names" with religious connotations. Baal simply means Lord or ruler, and so we hear of the Baal or the Baalat (Lady) of such-and-such a city. Similarly, a deity will be called Melek, meaning King. So, too, Adon; which means Lord or Master. Melqart meant King of the City.

To affirm Herodotus' reports of the Greeks' adoption of Egyptian deities, archaeological evidence in the 4th century (before our Common Era) shows that Athens was basically a center of Egyptian religion; and shrines to Isis (both public and private) were erected in many parts of Greece at that period.

In Magna Graecia, the monuments found in Catania in Sicily show that this city was a center of the worship of Egyptian deities. Southern Italy contained many temples of Isis, and the remains of statues, etc., found in Reggio, Puteoli, Pompeii, and Herculaneum prove that the worship of Egyptian deities must have been common.

The Ancient Egyptian religious practices were mirrored in Greece; for example, as confirmed by the Greek father of history, Herodotus, in the *Histories*, Book 2, [107]:

> ***It was the Egyptians too who originated, and taught the Greeks to use ceremonial meetings, processions, and processional offerings****: a fact that can be inferred from the obvious antiquity of such ceremonies in Egypt, compared with Greece, where they have been only recently introduced. The Egyptians meet in solemn assembly not once a year only, but on a number of occasions.*

Affirming Herodotus' statement, Plutarch states in *Moralia, Isis and Osiris* [378-9, 69],

> *Among the Greeks also many things are done which are similar to the Egyptian ceremonies in the shrines of Isis, and they do them at about the same time.*

In Rome, in the 1st century BCE, Isis was regarded as the principal deity of the city. Great buildings and temples were set up in her honor, filled with Egyptian objects, obelisks, altars, statues, etc., which were brought from

Egypt in order to make the shrines of Isis resemble those of her native country. Priestesses who professed to be well acquainted with the "mysteries" of Isis dwelt in or near these temples, and assisted in performing services and ceremonies in which large congregations participated.

In Ancient Egyptian cosmology, Isis represents the power responsible for the creation of all living creatures. Accordingly, Ancient Egyptians called her *Isis with the 10,000 Names/Attributes*. The "many names" of Isis were adopted throughout Greece and in Italy and beyond. Thus, the Greeks and Romans identified her frequently as Selene, Demeter, Ceres, and several other names. She was also regarded as Mother Earth; and as such, was the mother of all fertility, planting, crops, harvesting, and abundance. Some of her attributes caused her to be identified as Aphrodite, Juno, Nemesis, Fortuna, and Panthea.

The Ancient Egyptian religious practices associated with Isis and Osiris had made major strides in Italy. In Campania, an inscription dated at 105 (before our Common Era), was found in a temple of the Ancient Egyptian Sarapis (Sar-Apis) at Puteoli, which is evidence that the temple existed prior to that date. About 80 (before our Common Era) (in the time of Sulla), a College of the Servants of Isis (or Pastophori), was founded in Rome, and a temple was built in the city. In 44 (before our Common Era), a temple was built in Rome to honor Isis and Osiris; and a few decades later, the festival of these Egyptian deities was recognized in the public calendar.

The main festival in Italy corresponded exactly to the Ancient Egyptian festival that commemorated Osiris' murder and the finding of his body by Isis. As in Ancient Egypt, it opened in November with the singing of dirges and heartbreaking lamentations for the death of Osiris, which were, no doubt, based upon the compositions that were sung in Egypt at about the same time. Then, on the second day, scenes were enacted that represented the frantic grief and anxiety of those who went about searching for the body of Osiris. On the third day, Isis found the body of her husband, and there was great rejoicing in the temple. Grief gave place to gladness and tears to laughter; musicians of all kinds assembled and played their instruments; men and women danced; and everyone celebrated.

The Ancient Egyptian religious practices as they relate to the model story of Isis and Osiris spread all over southern Europe and into many parts of North Africa, and continued to be a religious power in these regions until the close of the 4th century (of our Common Era). These Ancient Egyptian ideas and beliefs survived in Christianity, whereby Mary the Virgin assumed the attributes of Isis the Everlasting Mother and the Babe Jesus assumed those of Horus.

[Read more about the testimonies of writers of antiquities regarding the spread of Ancient Egyptian colonies and influence throughout the whole world in *Ancient Egyptian Culture Revealed* and/or *Egyptian Romany: The Essence of Hispania;* both by Moustafa Gadalla.]

7.2 COSMIC SIGNIFICANCE OF EGYPTIAN FESTIVALS

As stated above in this chapter, all significant religious festivals in the Mediterranean basin were copies of

Ancient Egyptian ceremonies; and in most cases, only the Egyptian priesthood performed the required rituals.

During numerous Ancient Egyptian religious festivals, the participants fall back on the archetypal truth of their cosmic consciousness (As above so below, and as below so above). Every holy festival actualizes the archetypal holy cycle.

These holy cycles have become part of the calendar. More accurately, the calendar served to indicate when the cosmological powers (neteru/gods) were manifested, and their renewal cycles. All early Greek and Roman writers affirmed this Ancient Egyptian tradition, such as Plutarch, in his *Moralia Vol. V* (377,65):

> "... *They [the Egyptians] associate theological concepts with the seasonal changes in the surrounding atmosphere, or with the growth of the crops and seed-times and plowing*"

We will find the very same Egyptian principles being followed in other countries, as shown below.

7.3 QUEEN OF MARSHES

One of the most celebrated festivals in Ancient Egypt was the end of the 50-day period in which Isis hid with her baby son in the marshes. She and her son went into hiding in order to protect his son from being killed by the evil tyrant ruler Seth. As such, she is the Queen of the Marshes. Such a festival was described in extensive detail in Herodotus 2.59-60.

This beautiful Ancient Egyptian festival in the Nile Delta

has a practically duplicate festival at the Guadalquiver Delta in Spain, which is organized by the descendants of Egyptians, recognized as the 'Gitanos'.

The festival, which is described by some as "the most pagan", involves a pilgrimage to the edge of the great marsh of the Guadalquivir Delta for the Pentecost festival celebrating Isis in her names as:

> *The White Dove, Queen of the Marshes, the Virgin of the Dew, etc.*

Likewise, in present-day Egypt, the Apostles (Prophets) Festival in Egypt is held 50 days after Easter Saturday. This festival is of Ancient Egyptian origin. Pentecost signifies the period of the Khamaseen (meaning the Fifty) when the southerly hot and reddish sandstorms and winds are of frequent occurrence. This annual event commences on the day immediately following Good Friday (i.e. Easter (Light) Saturday), and ceases on the Day of Pentecost (or Whitesunday)—an interval of 50 days.

This Pentecostal event is related to the Ancient Egyptian allegory of Isis and Osiris: after Osiris was killed, Seth became the ruler of Egypt, and he went searching for the baby son Horus in order to kill him. The evil Seth ruled oppressively until he was dethroned 50 "days" later. Seth represents the color red and the oppressive weather that is dry, fiery, and arid. In other words, Seth represents the red, hot cloud of dust—Khamaseen. The festival commemorates the end of oppressive weather. The skies are no longer dusty and red. The skies are clear and white. During the oppressive 50 days, Isis hid with her baby son in the marshes. As such, she is the *Queen of the Marshes*.

7.4 LADY OF SORROW—[CRY ME A RIVER]

The Egyptians associate the beginning of the annual flood season with Isis, who began to weep after her soul mate Osiris, who ascended to heaven 40 days after his death. Egyptians associated Isis' first teardrop with the beginning of the rise of the Nile. Isis continued to weep, wishing for the lifeless Osiris to rise again. The Weeping Widow became, to the Egyptians, the **Lady of Sorrow**.

This religious festival was/is associated with a renewal cycle—the water cycle, where, symbolically, Isis regenerates/recreates Osiris (who represents the element of water) when 'he' evaporates and 'rises to heaven'—so to speak.

When there is no water, Isis ('Mother Earth') yearns for it.

Ancient Egyptian texts refer to Isis as:

> **"The Queen of earth.**
> **The Lady of the solid earth".**

The feminine principle of fertility is found in equating the Earth with Isis. But without water, no growth can occur. As we have seen, Isis, the female principle of intellect, has created the soul to animate the creation conception and bring it into life.

On another manifestation of that thought, we find that Isis, being Mother Earth, will generate water to fertilize the seeds in her womb—here being Mother Earth. Just as the intellectual aspect of Isis generated the soul, we likewise find Isis' role as the generator and life-giver of Osiris is shown in several of her 10,000 names; for we read that Isis is:

> **The Creatrix of the Nile Flood.**
> **Whose husband is the lord of the deep**
> **Whose husband is the inundation of the Nile.**
> **Who maketh the Nile to swell and overflow.**
> **Who maketh the Nile to swell in his season.**

When there is no water, Mother Earth yearns for it. The feminine principle of Isis therefore generates the water; and when the water disappears, Isis regenerates it.

The Eve of the 11th of the Ancient Egyptian month of Ba-oo-neh (18 June) is called "Leylet en-Nuqtah" (or the Night of the Tear Drop), as it commemorates the first drop that falls into the Nile, beginning the annual flood season. Astrologers calculate the precise moment when the "drop" is to fall, which is always in the course of the night of the 18th of June. This Ancient Egyptian celebration is recognized in northern Cairo as Mouled el-Embabi.

The Egyptian peasants all along the Nile Valley particularly welcomed this ancient festival. Diodorus of Sicily tells us how the husbandmen indulged in recreations of every kind and showed their gratitude to God for the benefits of the inundation. According to Heliodorus, it was one of the principal festivals of the Egyptians. Libanius asserts that these rites were deemed of so much importance by the Egyptians throughout the land that unless they were performed at the proper season, and in a becoming manner, by the persons appointed to this duty, they believed that the Nile would refuse to rise and inundate the land.

The Nile begins to rise about, or soon after, the period of the summer solstice. Two weeks after the first teardrop (i.e. from, or about, the 27th of the month Ba-oo-neh – 3rd of July), the incremental increases in the water level of the Nile were proclaimed daily in the streets of the city, as stated by Plutarch, and were continued by Baladi Egyptians until the Aswan High Dam was built in the 1960s.

One of the most compelling parts of the Egyptian Model Story of Isis and Osiris is how these two symbols relate to the flood season in Egypt. The Egyptians associated the beginning of the flood with Isis after her husband/soulmate Osiris ascended to heaven 40 days after his death, when she started weeping, begging her dead husband to rise again. Egyptians associated her first teardrop with the beginning of the rise of the Nile. Isis continued to weep, wishing for her husband to rise.

The beauty here is that Isis wishes her husband to rise from the dead, and the water of the Nile consequently rises, as well. It should be noted that the water of the Nile is symbolized by Osiris himself.

Plutarch described this relationship in his *Moralia, Vol. V* (366, 38A), as follows:

> ... *As the Egyptians regard the Nile as the effusion of Osiris, so they hold and believe the earth to be the body of Isis, not all of it, but so much of it as the Nile covers, fertilizing it and uniting with it. From this union they make Horus to be born...*

In other words, Isis recreates/regenerates Osiris from her tears every year. Her tears are blood red in color, which is the same color of the floodwaters, since this water comes as a result of the rainy season in Ethiopia, which erodes the silt of the Ethiopian highlands and carries it towards Egypt along the Blue Nile and other tributaries. So, Isis' tears represent this reddish color of the water during the flood season. In essence, **Isis is crying a river**—so to speak. The Christian faithful follow the same Ancient Egyptian traditions in their presentations of the statues of Mary with bloody teardrops coming out of her eyes.

7.5 ISIS: LADY OF ASSUMPTION

Isis, being Mother Earth, gets flooded by the rising water of the River Nile.

Isis becomes submerged underneath her own tears. As a result, the earth/land disappears underneath the water (i.e. the earth, being Isis, disappears) she rises to the Heavens.

The 15th day of August is a national holiday in many countries, commemorating the Ascension of the Virgin Mary to the heavens. On the very same day—the 15th of August – the Egyptians have commemorated, since ancient times, a very similar festival for Isis: the Ancient Egyptian Virgin Mother, called ***Bride of the Nile***.

In the Ancient Egyptian context, the Bride of the Nile is Isis—the Virgin Mother—and the River Nile is her soul mate Osiris. On the 15th of August, the Ancient Egyptian festival commemorates the end of the 50-day rainy period in Ethiopia, which causes the annual flooding of the Nile.

In this popular Egyptian allegory, Isis finished her crying over her soul mate Osiris in about the middle of August, which means that Isis had cried all the tears she had. It is at this point in time that the Egyptians (both ancient and modern) hold a festival, signifying the last teardrop from Isis, which will cause the peak of the flood level. It is during this celebration that the Egyptians throw an effigy of Isis into the waters, to symbolize that Isis drowned in her own tears—the River Nile itself.

Across the Mediterranean Sea from Egypt, every year on the eve of the 15th of August, a sacred musical drama is sung in the cathedral of Elche, Spain—a "mystery" on the disappearance and Assumption of the Virgin Mary, with the same words and music and the same stage properties that have been used since at least the 15th century.

The solemn procession is held on the 15th of August. It has been acknowledged by all that neither the procession nor the Mystery Play are purely church festivals, and that they pre-date Christianity.

The "historical" tradition associated with the Elche festival is very interesting. They say that in May 1266, or (as others say) in December 1370, an "ark" drifted to the coast of Spain. It was labeled "for Elche", and was found to contain an image of the Virgin Mary as well as the words, music, and ceremonial of a liturgical drama. [For more information about this and other related subjects, read *Egyptian Romany: Essence of Hispania* by Moustafa Gadalla.]

7.6 CELEBRATING HER 'BIRTHDAY'

In the normal course of events, the rising waters of the Nile starts receding and the submerged land is no longer so. The earth is visible again; a new *'birth'* for Earth and for Mother Earth/Isis.

In actuality, Isis NEVER dies. She emerges when the surrounding waters recedes.

The Ancient Egyptians celebrated that day as the *'birthday'* of Isis three days prior to the beginning of the Ancient Egyptian New Year. Isis' *birthday* in today's Latin Calendar is September 8th. Isis' birthday is one of five deities whose birthdays are celebrated prior the beginning of the Egyptian New Year.

The church celebrates the Nativity of the Virgin Mary on the same day as that of Isis. It is a national holiday throughout the countries of the Mediterranean Sea and Central and South Americas.

7.7 CELEBRATING OUR (HOLY) MOTHER OF THE SEA

As shown earlier, one of Isis' manifestations is Hathor/Astarte—like other Egyptian deities, she is also commonly known as Asera/Serah/Sarah, which means a **noble lady**.

To leave no doubt of her Egyptian origin, Aserah is always portrayed in her Egyptian form, with a crescent-and-disk on her headdress.

Hathor represents the matrix of the metaphysical spiritual principle, providing spiritual nourishment, healing, joy, lovemaking, music, and cheerfulness.

Hathor, as the symbol of spiritual nourishment, also plays an important role in the transformational (funerary) texts, furnishing the spiritual nourishment/guidance required by the soul of the deceased as it travels across the cosmic sea. Consequently, Hathor/Aserah is the Egyptian travel and sailing patroness; and, as a result, she appears in this role more often outside Egypt.

An Egyptian coffin text [coffin text no. 61] from the Middle Kingdom (2040-1783 BCE) describes her as Hathor:

> *the Lady who is said to 'hold the steering oars of . . . barks'.*

Hathor's head is therefore always depicted right above the stern of ships where the twin rudders (which expert pilots used to guide the vessel) were mounted.

In her role as a guardian of travelers, Hathor is called Astarte. Her temples were found at border cities, being she was a traveler patroness. Her temple at Cádiz, Spain was one of the major monuments at this holy city. The role of Astarte in Ancient Egypt is well documented. From small fragments from the time of Ramses II (1304-1237 BCE), the role of Astarte as patroness of overseas travel is evident. In one fragment, the role of Astarte as a seafaress patroness is clearly stated:

> *. . . Behold, Astarte dwelleth in the region of the sea . . .*"

To leave no doubt of her Egyptian origin, Astarte is

always portrayed in her Egyptian form with a crescent-and-disk on her headdress.

In another fragment, Renenutet addresses Astarte:

> *Behold, if thou bringest him tribute, he will be gracious unto*
> *thee. . .Therefore give him his tribute in silver, gold, lapis*
> *lazuli, and. . . wood.*
> *And she said unto the Ennead of gods:*
> *. . . the tribute of the sea; may he hearken unto us. . .*

During (and subsequent to) the turbulent times of the Reconquest, many people fled from the Iberian Peninsula to North Africa, Egypt, and France. The most prominent festival in southern France is held by the (Egyptian) Romany at the seaside by the Mediterranean Sea, towards the end of spring. The pilgrimage destination is the Church of **Notre Dame de La Mer**.

The name of the church in Ancient Egyptian language means : Notre (our holy/goddess), Dame (Da-me means 'the mother'), de La Mer (means water body/ sea—the same as in Spanish).

This Romany pilgrimage to the site of this church is the oldest in France.

The "historical" tradition associated with this Romany festival had a solid connection to Egypt. According to tradition, a dark-skinned Egyptian maiden called St. Sarah arrived in a tiny boat without oars or sail, together with two white-skinned maidens whose names are Mary

Salome and Mary Jacobe. Their boat is said to have landed on this part of the Mediterranean coast, having drifted across the Mediterranean Sea, about 42 CE.

The "name" of the center stage character of this festival is also significant. Her name—Sarah—is an Ancient Egyptian word that is the feminine form of Sar which equals a person of high/noble status. Sarah therefore means the **Noble Lady**, in the Ancient Egyptian language. In Ancient Egyptian traditions, Saint Sarah is Hathor —Patroness of Travelers by Water. Her name, Sarah, is consistent with her being **Our Holy Mother of the Sea**, as stated above.

Similar accounts of an ark drifting to the shores of the Iberian Peninsula are found in many places. Such accounts are found, among other places, at Elche, Spain and Santiago de Compostela.

It is no accident that the theme of a (woman) saint and her two guardian angels (Mary Salome and Mary Jacobe) that we find in southern France is also found at Elche and numerous places where these dark/tanned skin people—the descendants of the Egyptian Pharaohs—are to be found.

The "Two Marys" are the Twin Sisters Isis and Nephthys—the two accompanying guiding angels described earlier in this book.

CHAPTER 8 : THE MIGHTY HEART

8.1 MARY ISIS: THE CURE-ALL

In this chapter, we will present the role of Isis as the cure-all, showing how mankind is always seeking her aid.

Isis the female principle is not only responsible for conceiving and bringing to life all forms of creation, but what the female principle Isis brought forth, she protects and cares for and feeds and nourishes, and she uses her power graciously and successfully, for all those who seek her aid. Being the divine mother, she is the cure-all.

The populace of Egypt looked upon Isis as a patroness whose solicitude extended over the entire range of human needs. To those in need, no other divine figure equaled the status of Isis the Virgin Mother.

Isis as the Queen of Osiris and Mother of the God (i.e., Horus), and her loving care, made her Queen of Heaven. Her protection was eagerly sought throughout Egypt, and spread throughout the world.

She became the great and beneficent netert (goddess) and mother, whose influence and love pervaded all heaven and earth and the Other World; and she became the personification of the great feminine, creative power that conceived and brought forth every living creature and thing, from the deities in heaven to man on the Earth and insects on the ground.

She was the personification of all tilled lands, the benevolent spirit of the fields, and the netert of the harvest. What she brought forth, she protected and cared for and fed and nourished, and she employed her life towards using her power graciously and successfully—not only in creating new beings, but in restoring to life those who were dead. Throughout the *Book of the Coming Forth by Day/Light* [known mistakenly as the *Book of the Dead*], Isis is spoken of as a giver of life and food for the dead. Her countless attributes inspired the Ancient Egyptians to call her Isis With the 10,000 Names/Attributes.

The populace of Egypt looked upon the Virgin as a patroness whose solicitude extended over the entire range of human needs. She bestowed her own divine favors, and was indiscriminate in the way that she gave to all who asked. To those in need, no other divine figure equaled the status of the Virgin Mother; and no other sacred symbol so calmed their anxieties and indulged their fantasies. She was the guarantee of man's soul for having refused to admit his body.

Diodorus of Sicily, in *Book I*, [25. 2-6], describes the same qualities of the (Egyptian) Virgin—Isis:

> *"As for Isis, the Egyptians say that she was the discoverer of many health-giving drugs and was greatly versed in the science of healing; consequently, now that she has attained immortality, she finds her greatest*

delight in the healing of mankind and gives aid in their sleep to those who call upon her, plainly manifesting both her very presence and her beneficence towards men who ask for her help. In proof of this, as they say, they advance not legends, as the Greeks do, but manifest facts; for practically the entire inhabited world is their witness, in that it eagerly contributes to the honors of Isis because she manifests herself in healings.

For standing above the sick in their sleep she gives them aid for their diseases and works remarkable cures upon such as submit themselves to her; and many who have been despaired of by their physicians because of the difficult nature of their malady are restored to health by her, while numbers who have altogether lost the use of their eyes or of some other part of their body, whenever they turn for help to this goddess, are restored to their previous condition. Furthermore, she discovered also the drug which gives immortality, by means of which she not only raised from the dead her son Horus",..

Isis was regarded as a great magician, and the ancient Egyptian papyri contain several allusions to her magical powers. From a number of passages in the texts of various periods, we learn that Isis possessed great skill in the working of magic, and several examples of the manner in which she employed it are well known. She knew how to weave spells and how to fashion magical figures and she possessed the knowledge of all the secret hidden names of all the divine powers and of all the spirits both good and bad. She used them in such away that each of them was compelled to do her will. At her bidding, the powers of nature ceased or modified their operations, and she could make everything, both animate and inanimate, perform her will.

Isis was well skilled in the use of words of power, and is known as:

> **Mistress of spells.**
> **Lady of Words of Power.**

One of the most powerful amulets known to the Egyptians was the object thet, which carried with it the influence of her blood, magical powers, and words of power. It is most probably a conventional representation of the uterus, with its ligatures, and the vagina. An analogy suggests that the amulet, the all-powerful symbol of Isis, represents some organ of her body.

Isis represents the permanence principle. She appealed to all as the type and symbol of all that is greatest and best in woman in her character of the unselfish, true, tender, loving, and eternal World Mother.

8.2 HOMAGE TO THE QUEEN

Isis' worshipers are not limited to the land of Egypt, but are found everywhere. In the *Golden Ass of Apuleius of Madaura,* Lucius prays to Isis using these words:

> *"Queen of heaven, —the kindly mother from whom in the beginning spring the fruits of earth, who, rejoicing to have found thy daughter, didst take from men their bestial provender of old-world acorns and show forth to them a sweeter food, and now thou honourest exceedingly the soil of Eleusis; or beest thou Venus, the*

> *heavenly one, who at the first beginning of things didst unite the diversity of the sexes in the power of Love that is born of thee, and, after thou hadst brought to birth the race of man that shall endure from generation to generation; or with gentle healing dost bring relief to women in travail and hast reared such multitudes, thou that with thy tender feminine light dost illumine the walls of all cities and with thy moist fires dost nurture the springing seeds, and dispensest thy beams that shift and change with the changes of the sun—by whatever name, by whatever rite, in whatever semblance man may invoke thee."*

To this prayer, Isis made answer:

> *"I am come I, nature's mother, mistress of all the elements, the first-begotten offspring of all the ages, of deities mightiest, queen of the dead, first of heaven's denizens, in whose aspect are blent the aspects of all divine energies. With my rod I rule the shining heights of heaven, the health-giving breezes of the sea, the mournful silence of the Underworld. The whole earth worships my godhead, one and individual, under many a changing shape, with varied rites and by many diverse names."*

A homage to Isis, the Queen of heaven and Earth, reads:

The divine one, with the 10,000 attributes:

Isis:

> *The Queen of all the divine forces.*
> *The lady of the beginning of time.*

The maker of the sunrise.
The lady of heaven.
The Light-giver in heaven with Re.
The Queen of earth.
The Lady of the solid earth.
The Blazing flame.
The mother of the god.
The Bestower of life.
The Lady of life.
The Lady of joy and gladness.
The Lady of Love.
The Weaver and fuller.
The Whose son is the lord of the earth.
Beloved in all lands.

As for Egypt, the home of Isis, the silent majority never changed the old traditions, and her attributes or so-called names have never died; for she is:

7 Banat—the seven maidens, namely Hathors—Venus.
Setna Aisha—the lady of Bread—the bestower of life.
Setna Fattma—the lady that weaned her child.
Setna Sekina—the lady of serenity.
Setna Mariam—the beloved mother (Mari-Om).
Setna Zeneib—the highest house (zenith-b).
Setna Ttahra—the Virgin—the pure.
Setna Nafisa—the dearest—bestower of breath, giving life.
Set el Kol—the lady of all—the lady of the universe.

Beloved in all Lands!

APPENDIX 1: EGYPTIAN COSMOLOGY AND ALLEGORIES

The totality of Egyptian civilization was built upon a complete and precise understanding of universal laws. This profound understanding manifested itself in a consistent, coherent, and interrelated system where art, science, philosophy and religion were intertwined, and were employed simultaneously in a single organic Unity.

Egyptian cosmology is based on coherent scientific and philosophical principles. The cosmological knowledge of Ancient Egypt was expressed in a story form, which is a superior means for expressing both physical and metaphysical concepts. Any good writer or lecturer knows that stories are better than exposition for explaining the behavior of things, because the relationships of parts to each other, and to the whole, are better maintained by the mind. Information alone is useless unless it is transformed into understanding.

The Egyptian sagas transformed common factual nouns and adjectives (indicators of qualities) into proper but conceptual nouns. These were, in addition, personified so that they could be woven into coherent and meaningful narratives. Personification is based on their knowledge that man was made in the image of God and, as such, man represented the created image of all creation.

Allegories are an intentionally chosen means for communicating knowledge. Allegories dramatize cosmic laws, principles, processes, and relationships and functions, and express them in an easy-to-understand way. Once the inner meanings of the allegories have been revealed, they become marvels of simultaneous scientific and philosophical completeness and conciseness. The more they are studied, the richer they become. The 'inner dimension' of the teachings embedded into each story are capable of revealing several layers of knowledge, according to the stage of development of the listener. The "secrets" are revealed as one evolves higher. The higher we get, the more we see. It is always there.

The Egyptians (Ancient and present-day Baladi) did/do not believe their allegories as historical facts. They believed IN them, in the sense that they believed in the truth beneath the stories.

We have shown, earlier, three different subjects that are explained in story forms, using four personified concepts: Isis, Osiris, Horus, and Seth:

> 1 – The solar and lunar principles as represented by Isis and Osiris.
>
> 2 – Numerology and trigonometry as described into the relationship between the father [Osiris], mother [Isis], and son [Horus] are analogous to the right-angle triangle 3:4:5.
>
> 3 – The four elements of the world (water [Osiris], fire [Seth], earth [Isis], and air [Horus]), as quoted from Plutarch's *Moralia Vol. V.*

The Egyptian well-crafted mystery plays are an intentionally chosen means for communicating knowledge. Meaning and the mystical experience are not tied to a literal interpretation of events. Once the inner meanings of the narratives have been revealed, they become marvels of simultaneous scientific and philosophical completeness and conciseness. The more they are studied, the richer they become. And, rooted in the narrative as it is, the part can never be mistaken for the whole; nor can its functional significance be forgotten or distorted.

APPENDIX 2: THE UNIVERSAL EGYPTIAN ALLEGORY—ISIS AND OSIRIS

The Egyptian allegory of Isis and Osiris explains practically all facets of life.

The following is a shortened version of the story of the Isis and Osiris Egyptian allegory, with emphasis on the role of Isis as the divine female's principle, manifestations, and applications. The narrative is shown in broken segments, each followed by a concise metaphysical evaluation of each segment.

This narrative is compiled from Ancient Egyptian temples, tombs, and papyri, dated more than 3,000 years before Christianity, and goes as follows:

The self-created Atam/Atum begat the twins Shu and Tefnut who, in turn, gave birth to Nut (the sky/spirit) and Geb (the earth/matter).

The union of Nut (spirit) and Geb (matter) produced four offspring:

Osiris, Isis, Seth, and Nepthys.

>> **Like the biblical Jesus, Osiris symbolizes the divine in a mortal form, combining both spirit (Nut) and matter (Geb).**

The Egyptian allegory goes that Osiris married Isis, and Seth married NepthysNebt. Osiris became King of the land (Egypt) after marrying Isis.

>> **The story sets the basis for the matrilineal/matriarchal society. Isis is the legal heiress.**

Osiris brought civilization and spirituality to the people, enabling them to achieve prosperity. He gave them a body of laws to regulate their conduct, settled their disputes justly, and instructed them in the science of spiritual development.

Having civilized Egypt, he traveled around the world to spread the same instructions. Wherever Osiris went, he brought peace and learning to the people.

>> **Osiris, representing the universal soul, is always in motion. He travels, while the feminine principle Isis is the symbol of stability. He spread the thoughts of Isis throughout the whole world.**

>> **There are vivid similarities between the two evangelists (Osiris and Jesus):**

- **The divine son comes down from heaven.**
- **God came down to earth to guide the world.**
- **Both had traveled to spread the word.**

When Osiris returned from his mission, he was greeted with a royal feast. Osiris was tricked by Seth—the evil one—and his accomplices into lying down inside a makeshift coffin. The evil group quickly closed and sealed the chest, and threw it into the Nile. Seth became the new pharaoh as the coffin containing the lifeless body of Osiris flowed into the Mediterranean Sea.

>> **Both Jesus and Osiris were betrayed by dinner guests (Jesus by Judas, and Osiris by Seth) at their own privately-held banquets.**

Upon receiving the news of the fate of Osiris and his disappearance, Isis was in grief and vowed never to rest until she found her lost beloved Osiris—for her heart could not live without her soul mate. The power of love and devotion made her move. There would be nothing that could stand in her way. She will do whatever it takes because she must reunite with her soul—Osiris.

Isis searched everywhere, accosting everyone she met, including children.

>> **1. This reflects a total devotion and commitment to finding and pursuing the spiritual path that will reunite her with Osiris, who is described in the Egyptian texts as *'the Manifester of Truth'*.**

>> **2. Isis was not passive, but was very active in searching everywhere and accosting everyone she met, including children. Chil-**

dren represent the power of divination, which is a mode of gaining knowledge that is beyond our limited human senses.

The story continues that the coffin of Osiris was taken by the waves to the shoreline of a foreign land. A tree sprang up and grew around it, enclosing the body of Osiris in its trunk. The tree grew large, beautiful, and fragrant.

News of this magnificent tree came to the king of this alien land, who ordered that it be cut down and its trunk brought to him. He utilized the trunk as a pillar in his house without knowing the great secret it contained within.

>> **This refers to the Tree of Life, with all that that implies. It is also a reference to the Tet (Djed) pillar of Osiris.**

In Christianity, this became the Christmas tree.

Isis had a revelation, in her dreams, that the body of Osiris was in this foreign land. So she immediately traveled there.

When she arrived, she dressed as a commoner, befriended the queen's handmaidens, and was able to get a job in the palace as a nurse of the baby prince, so as to be close to the wooden pillar that contained the body of her beloved Osiris.

>> **This is remarkable, because here is Isis . . . the Queen of Egypt . . . serving OTHERS without exception, to achieve UNION with her love Osiris.**

Later, Isis confessed to the queen her identity and the purpose of her mission. Isis then asked the king for the pillar to be given to her. The king granted her request and she cut deep into the trunk and took out the chest.

Isis returned back to Egypt with the chest containing the lifeless body of Osiris. She hid the body in the marshes of the Nile Delta.

Any woman who truly loves her husband is considered to be like Isis, and has the power of awakening him into greater life, as Horus. Father S.J. Vann likened the awakening of Christ by Mary Magdalene, as he emerged from his tomb, to Isis awakening Osiris from the dead.

The comparison between the two cases is illuminated in the "Lament for Osiris", in which Isis and her sister Nephthys bewailed

Osiris death and pleaded with him to come back to life. The text for this duet was derived from a much older lamentation.

"Lament for Osiris" was described by Andrew Lang to "have the power to stir our deepest emotions":

> Sing we Osiris dead,
> Lament the fallen head:
> The light has left the world, the world is gray.
> Athwart the starry skies
> The web of darkness flies,
> And Isis weeps Osiris passed away.
> Your tears, ye stars, ye fires, ye rivers shed,
> Weep, children of the Nile, weep for your lord is dead!
> Softly we tread, our measured footsteps falling
> Within the sanctuary sevenfold;
> Soft on the dead that liveth are we calling:
> 'Return, Osiris, from thy Kingdom cold!
> Return to them that worship thee of old.
> Within the court divine
> The sevenfold sacred shrine
> We pass, while echoes of the temple walls
> Repeat the long lament
> The sound of sorrow sent
> Far up within the imperishable halls,
> Where, each in other's arms, the sisters weep,
> Isis and Nephthys o'er his unawakening sleep.
>
> Softly we tread, our measured footsteps falling
> Within the sanctuary sevenfold;
> Soft on the dead that liveth are we calling:
> 'Return, Osiris, from thy kingdom cold!
> Return to them that worship thee of old.'
> O dweller in the west,
> Lover and lordliest,
> Thy love, thy sister Isis, calls thee home!
> Come from thy chamber dun,
> Thou master of the sun,
> Thy Shadowy chamber far below the foam!
> With weary wings and spent
> Through all the firmament,
> Through all the horror-haunted ways of hell,
> I seek thee near and far,
> From star to wandering star,
> Free with the dead that in Amenti dwell.

> I search the height, the deep, the lands, the skies,
> Rise from the dead and live, our lord Osiris, rise!

Isis wanted her husband to live on. The lifeless body of Osiris was never going to stop Isis; for where there is a will, there is a way. She therefore wanted to have his son by any means.

She used her magical powers to transform herself into a dove. Drawing the essence of Osiris from him, she conceived a child—Horus.

In other words, Isis was impregnated by the holy ghost of Osiris.

>> 1. **This action symbolizes reincarnation and spiritual rebirth—a key to understanding the Egyptian belief in life after death.**

At her most specific role, Isis is the womb out of which the new Osirian life rises after death.

>> 2. The conception of Horus by Isis by no living man is the oldest documented version of an Immaculate Conception. The role of Isis in the Egyptian Model Story and the story of the Virgin Mary are strikingly similar; for both were able to conceive without male impregnation, and, as such, Isis was revered as the Virgin Mother.

3. On a purely intellectual level, we see here that the female principle (Isis) is creating the essence of the male Osiris so as to be impregnated by him. In other words, the female principle of intellect generated the male principle of soul so that an offspring could be born and the creation process could continue. This Egyptian thinking gives a deeper meaning to the Immaculate Conception.

When Seth heard about the new child, Horus, he went to kill the newborn. Hearing that Seth was coming, Isis was told to take Horus to a secluded spot in the marshes of the Nile Delta, where she kept him safe and raised him.

During his early years, Horus, the child, was stung to death by a scorpion, and Isis was able to use a magic formula to bring her son back to life.

>> **This is the source of the story in which Herod, upon hearing about the birth of the biblical Jesus, set out to destroy all the newborn males.**

In the New Testament, the angel of the Lord says to Joseph, "*Arise and take the young child and his mother and flee into Egypt.*"

The story continues that one night (while Isis was caring for Horus in hiding and when the moon was full), the evil Seth and his accomplices found the chest containing the lifeless body of Osiris and cut him into fourteen pieces. The number fourteen symbolizes the number of days required to shape a full moon.

Osiris represents the lunar principle in the universe, and is known as Osiris the Moon.

\>\> **The moon reflects the power of the sun. Isis, the female principle, represents the sun. Osiris, the male, represents the moon.**

When Isis heard about how Seth and his accomplices cut Osiris into different pieces and scattered them throughout the land, her job was to search near and far so as to collect and put the broken pieces back together.

\>\> **1. One remembers and recollects in order to heal and in order never to forget. The actions of Isis to recollect and to remember involve putting the pieces together so as to achieve unity with the Divine.**

\>\> **2. By recollecting and remembering the story of Isis and Osiris, we keep in our hearts a tale that expresses, in Joseph Campbell's words, "*the immanence of divinity in the phenomenal forms of the universe.*"**

\>\> **3. 'To bind or tie together' is the meaning of the "Latin" word RELIGIO, which is the root of the word 'religion'.**

During her search for the broken pieces, Isis sought the assistance of Anubis, the divine guide, to serve as her guide and guard. She also sought the help of Thoth, who provided knowledge and wisdom in her spiritual path.

\>\> **1. This signifies the need for spiritual guidance in your journey. Anbu represents (like a dog) the (spiritual) pathfinder.**

2. Knowledge and wisdom, as represented by Thoth, are needed in traveling the spiritual path.

Isis, with the help of others, collected all the pieces all except the phallus, which had been swallowed by a fish in the Nile. She then reunited the dismembered body of Ausar and, with the help of others, wrapped it in linen bandages and mummified it.

Thoth, Isis, and Horus performed the Ceremony of **Opening the Mouth** upon the mummy, and Osiris was brought back to life as the Judge and King of the Dead (the past), while Horus was to take his place as king of the living (the present).

>> **This represents the everlasting perpetual cycle of spiritual power on Earth: The King is dead (Osiris); Long live the King (Horus).**

As soon as Horus had grown to manhood, he challenged Seth for the right to the throne in what was called the Great Quarrel/Struggle in the Wilderness. There are a series of battles between Horus and Seth. Such illustrates how life is a continuous quest for the divine within ourselves, as symbolized by Horus and Seth.

The archetypal inner struggle in the Egyptian model is symbolized in the struggle between Horus and Seth. It is the archetypal struggle between opposing forces. Horus, in this context, is the divine man, born of nature, who must do battle against Seth, his own kin, who represents the power of opposition and not evil in the narrow sense. Seth represents the concept of opposition in all aspects of life (physically and metaphysically).

>> **This actually represents the inner struggle within each of us—as symbolized by the duality of Horus and Seth.**

Finally, both Horus and Seth went to the council of neteru (gods/goddesses) to determine who should rule. Both presented their cases. The council of neteru decided that Horus should rule over the habitable/populated areas and Seth should rule over the deserts/wastelands.

>> **This shows the concept and application of conflict resolution by jury trial, etc.**

The Isis and Osiris allegory shows us what love is and how TRUE LOVE conquers ALL.

APPENDIX 3: HEART AND SOUL—METAPHYSICAL REFLECTIONS

We have seen how the intellectual, loving heart of Isis conceived the creation plan and how Isis next brought the creation plan to life by conceiving the soul as the divine male principle. Yet, life is cyclical in its nature, and requires renewal and rebirth. Isis the female is constantly renewing life to the soul so that creation may continue on and on. The heart of Isis cannot live without the soul (being the male principle—Osiris).

As such, Isis and Osiris are the heart and the soul of the universe.

<u>The Heart</u>

The 'divine' heart, though connected in some mysterious way with each individual's physical heart, is not a thing of flesh and blood. Unlike the English 'heart', its nature is more intellectual than emotional, but whereas the intellect cannot gain real knowledge of The Divinity, the divine heart is capable of knowing the essences of all things; and when illumined by faith and knowledge, reflects the whole content of the divine mind.

The purified divine heart is the part of mankind that partakes of the essence of divinity.

The heart is that organ of perception which is capable of knowing all levels of reality, and of knowing the Whole as well as the parts. It may be that what the heart can know is the most a human being can know, and that is infinite.

The heart corresponds to *conscience;* and as such is identified with the totality of all the organs of knowledge.

The heart can be understood as the totality of qualitative, subconscious faculties which function in a unified way.

The heart can be understood as the center of the unconscious; the potential integrative power at our core.

The heart is the symbol for contemplation and inner metaphysical contact.

The heart contains a point of contact with the infinite dimension of Spirit, the source of all qualities.

To keep The Divine present in our hearts means that The Divine will become our reality. This Essence will become our essence. This Power will become our power. This Wholeness is our wholeness.

The heart is the point at which the individual human being is closest to the Divine Reality.

The Soul

The heart contains the soul—Breath of Life.

The beginning of the breath is as a divine emanation from potentiality to actuality proceeding without intermission or stint until the form is completed and perfected.

There is one single breath which accounts for the origin of the others; and this breath arises in the heart, passing thence into the principal centers of the body and lingering in them long enough to enable them to impart to it their respective temperamental properties.

It is this 'principal' breath associated with the heart that is identified with the force of life itself and is the link between the corporeal and the subtle and spiritual aspects of man's being. It is human breath which renders possible the perfect equilibrium and balance of the elements, the necessary condition for the manifestation of the Intellect.

The breath acts as the link between the physical and the psychic and spiritual worlds and plays a basic role not only in the physiological functions of the human being but also in his deliverance from the life of the body.

Purification of The Heart and Soul—Will and Way

The heart contains a point of contact with the infinite dimension of Soul, the source of all qualities. If we can allow Soul instead of ego to rule our hearts, a new life flows in. At this stage, we begin to purify ourselves of mental distractions and projections. We dissolve self-images and our narcissistic fictions. We learn to keep our thought processes in alignment with the Divine Reality through a more conscious relationship with it. We begin to see the Divine Reality more clearly in the multiplicity of forms.

The heart can be understood as the totality of qualitative, subconscious faculties which function in a unified way. Once activated, these faculties support and illuminate each other, much as eye-hand coordination is superior to either touch or sight alone. Although these functions seem to be separate, they serve a unifying purpose; which is to know unity beyond multiplicity. They are the subtle nervous system's means of realizing unity.

The fathoming of the human heart and the disclosure of the spiritual qualities it contains is the work of all life, art, spirituality. Our purpose in life is to know the heart without the veils of our fears, preoccupations, desires, and strategies. A human heart is the hologram of the seen and unseen universes; the part that reflects the whole.

The **purification of the heart** is a comprehensive education that has physical, intellectual, psychological, and moral dimensions. And yet, all this work is more effective if it can proceed within the boundless context of the heart.

To achieve the goal of becoming Isis, one must achieve purity of heart. The aspirant, in the Egyptian model, learns to purify his inner self by taming vices and practicing the opposites of such vices in society. Knowledge is gained by both the mind and acquired by experience.

Inner purification must be completed by practicing good social behavior in ordinary daily life. Every action impresses itself upon the heart. The inward being of a person is really the reflection of his deeds and actions. Doing good deeds thus establishes good inner qualities and the virtues impressed upon the heart, in turn, govern the actions of the limbs. As each act, thought, and deed makes an image on the heart, it becomes an attribute of the person.

This maturation of the soul through acquired attributes leads to progressive mystical visions and the ultimate unification with the Divine. Reciprocally, the knowledge obtained by both intellect and intuition is the source of virtue that must be practiced in ordinary life. The struggle for virtue and the vision of the Divine are all aspects of a single progressive achievement during the course of which the aspirant becomes more wise, until he achieves the totality of being that simultaneously entails mystical vision and ordinary piety. [More details about this subject is found in *Egyptian Mystics: Seekers of The Way* by Moustafa Gadalla.]

GLOSSARY

Animism – The concept that all things in the universe are animated (energized) by life forces. This concurs, scientifically, with kinetic theory, where each minute particle of any matter is in constant motion – i.e. energized with life forces.

attributes – the Divine qualities and meanings that are the real causative factors of manifested creations.

Baladi – local; a term used to describe the present native silent majority in Egypt, which adheres to the Ancient Egyptian traditions, under a thin layer of Islam.

BCE – Before Common Era. Also noted in other references as BC.

Book of Coming Forth By Light (Per-em-hru) – consists of over 100 chapters of varying lengths, which are closely related to the so-called Pyramid Texts at Saqqara. These texts are found on papyrus scrolls that were wrapped in the mummy swathings of the deceased and buried with him.

Book of the Dead – see Book of Coming Forth By Light.

CE – Common Era. Also noted in other references as AD.

Copt – is derived from the Greek rendering for an Egyptian. The Arabs, after 641 CE, labeled only the Christian population as Copts. As a result, the term 'Coptic' took on a different meaning by the 7th century.

cosmology – The study of the origin, creation, structure, and orderly operation of the universe as a whole, and of its related parts.

Duat/Tuat – (Ancient Egypt) the Underworld where the soul goes through transformation leading to resurrection.

matriarchy – a society/state/organization whose descent, inheritance, and governance are traced through the females. It is the woman who transmits political rights, and the husband she chooses then acts as her executive agent.

matrilineal – a society whose descent, inheritance, and governance are based on descent through the maternal line.

mysticism – consists of ideas and practices that lead to union with the Divine. Union is described more accurately as togetherness, joining, arriving, conjunction, and the realization of God's uniqueness.

neter/netert – a divine principle/function/attribute of the One Great God. Incorrectly translated as 'god/goddess'.

papyrus – could mean either: 1) A plant that is used to

make a writing surface. 2) Paper, as a writing medium. 3) The text written on it, such as "Leyden Papyrus".

Pyramid Texts – a collection of transformational (funerary) literature that was found in the tombs of the 5th and 6th Dynasties (2465-2150 BCE).

Re – represents the primeval, cosmic, creative force. His hidden name is Amen, which means 'secret'. All neteru (gods, goddesses) who took part in the creation process are aspects of Re. Therefore, Re is often linked with other neteru such as Atam-Re, Re-Harakhte, etc.

Ostracon – Term used by archaeologists to refer to shards of pottery or flakes of limestone bearing texts and drawings.

sacred geometry – The process by which all figures are to be drawn or created by using only a straight line (not even a ruler) and a compass (i.e. without measurement, dependent on proportion only).

stanza – a group of lines of verse forming one of the divisions of a poem or song. It typically has a regular pattern in the number of lines and the arrangement of meter and rhyme.

stele (plural: stelae) – stone or wooden slab or column inscribed with commemorative texts.

Thoth – represents the Divine aspects of wisdom and intellect. It was Thoth who uttered the words that created the world, as commanded by Re. Thoth is represented as the messenger of the neteru (gods/goddesses), of writing, language, and knowledge.

zodiac – An imaginary belt in the heavens extending for about eight degrees on either side of the apparent path of the sun and including the paths of the moon and the principal planets. It is divided into 12 equal parts or signs; each named for a different constellation.

SELECTED BIBLIOGRAPHY

Ameen, Ahmed. *The Egyptian Customs, Traditions and Expressions.* Cairo, 1999 [Arabic text].

Baines, John and Jaromir Málek. *Atlas of Ancient Egypt,* New York, 1994.

Bleeker, C.J. *Egyptian Festivals: Enactments of Religious Renewal.* Leiden, 1967.

Breasted, James Henry. *Ancient Records of Egypt,* 3 Vols. Chicago, USA, 1927.

Budge, E.A. Wallis. *Amulets and Superstitions.* New York, 1978.

Budge, E.A. Wallis. *Cleopatra's Needles and Other Egyptian Obelisks.* London, 1926.

Budge, E.A. Wallis. *The Decrees of Memphis and Canopis,* 3 Vols. London, 1904.

Budge, Sir E. A. Wallis. *Egyptian Language: Easy Lessons in Egyptian Hieroglyphics.* New York, 1983.

Budge, E.A. Wallis. *Egyptian Magic.* New York, 1971.

Budge, E.A. Wallis. *Egyptian Religion: Egyptian Ideas of the Future Life*. London, 1975.

Budge, E.A. Wallis. *From Fetish to God in Ancient Egypt*. London, 1934.

Budge, E.A. Wallis. *The Gods of the Egyptians*, 2 volumes. New York, 1969.

Budge, Wallis. *Osiris & The Egyptian Resurrection* (2 volumes). New York, 1973.

Catholic Encyclopedia, Online Edition, 1999. http://www.newadvent.org/cathen/.

Clement Stromata Book V, chapter IV [www.piney.com/Clement-Stromata-Five.html]

Diodorus of Sicily. *Books I, II, & IV*, tr. By C.H. Oldfather. London, 1964.

Egyptian Book of the Dead (The Book of Going Forth by Day), The Papyrus of Ani. USA, 1991.

Erman, Adolf. *Life in Ancient Egypt*. New York, 1971.

Farouk Ahmed Moustafa. *The Mouleds: A Study in the Popular Customs and Traditions in Egypt*. Alexandria, 1981 [Arabic text].

Findlen, Paula, Ed. *Athanasius Kircher: The Last Man Who Knew Everything*. New York, 2004.

Gadalla, Moustafa:
– *Ancient Egyptian Culture Revealed*. USA, 2007.
– *Egyptian Cosmology: The Animated Universe* – 2nd edition. USA, 2001.

– *Egyptian Divinities: The All Who Are THE ONE*. USA, 2001.
– *Egyptian Harmony: The Visual Music*. USA, 2000.
– *Egyptian Mystics: Seekers of the Way*. USA, 2003.
– *The Ancient Egyptian Roots of Christianity*. USA, 2007.
– *Egyptian Rhythm: The Heavenly Melodies*. USA, 2002.
– *Egyptian Romany: The Essence of Hispania*. USA, 2004.
– *Historical Deception: The Untold Story of Ancient Egypt*. USA, 1999.

Gilsenan, Michael. *Saint and Sufi in Modern Egypt*. Oxford, 1973.

Godwin, Joscelyn. *Athanasius Kircher: A Renaissance Man and the Quest for Lost Knowledge*. London, 1979.

Greek Orthodox Archdiocese of America website. www.goarch.org. 2002.

Hare, Tom. *Remembering Osiris*. Stanford, CA, USA, 1999.

Herodotus. *The Histories*. Tr. By Aubrey DeSelincourt. London, 1996.

Kastor, Joseph. *Wings of the Falcon, Life and Thought of Ancient Egypt*. USA, 1968.

Kircher, Athanasius. *Oedipus Aegyptiacus* (3 vols.), Rome, 1652-4.

Maxwell-Stuart, P.G., Ed. *The Occult in Early Modern Europe*. New York, USA, 1999.

Nicholson, Reynold A. *The Mystics of Islam*. New York, 1975.

Piankoff, Alexandre. *The Tomb of Ramesses VI*. New York, 1954.

Piankoff, Alexandre. *Mythological Papyri*. New York, 1957.

Piankoff, Alexandre. *The Litany of Re*. New York, 1964.

Piankoff, Alexandre. *The Pyramid of Unas Texts*. Princeton, NJ, USA, 1968.

Piankoff, Alexandre. *The Shrines of Tut-Ankh-Amon Texts*. New York, 1955.

Plato. *The Collected Dialogues of Plato including the Letters*. Edited by E. Hamilton & H. Cairns. New York, 1961.

Plotinus. *The Enneads*, in 6 volumes, Tr. By A.H. Armstrong. London, 1978.

Plotinus. *The Enneads*, Tr. By Stephen MacKenna. London, 1991.

Plutarch. *De Iside Et Osiride*. Tr. By J. Gwyn Griffiths. Wales, U.K., 1970.

Plutarch. *Plutarch's Moralia, Volume V*. Tr. by Frank Cole Babbitt. London, 1927.

Pritchard, James B., Ed. *Ancient Near Eastern Texts*. Princeton, NJ, USA, 1955.

Shafer, Byron E. (Ed.). *Religion in Ancient Egypt*. Ithaca, NY, USA, 1991.

Shah, Idries. *The Sufis*. New York, 1964.

Sicilus, Diodorus. *Vol 1*. Tr. by C.H. Oldfather. London.

Wilkinson, J. Gardner. *The Ancient Egyptians: Their Life and Customs*. London, 1988.

Several Internet sources.

Numerous references in Arabic language.

SOURCES AND NOTES

The author is extremely knowledgeable in several languages, such as Egyptian and Arabic tongues. He is also very knowledgeable in Islam, being born-Moslem in Egypt and subjected to Islamic studies all his life.

References to sources in the previous section, Selected Bibliography are only referred to for the facts, events, and dates—not for their interpretations of such information.

It should be noted that if a reference is made to one of the author Moustafa Gadalla's books, that each of his book contains appendices for its own extensive bibliography as well as detailed Sources and Notes.

Chapter 1: The Mother of Creation

1.1 Her Name
Gadalla [Cosmology, Divinities], Plutarch, Budge [all books]

1.2 The Universal Womb
Gadalla [Cosmology, Divinities], Plutarch, Budge [all books], Kastor, Piankoff [all books]

1.3 The One and All—Atam

Gadalla [Cosmology, Divinities], Plutarch, Budge [all books], Kastor, Piankoff [all books]

1.4 Ra: The Manifested Atam—Atam-Re
Gadalla [Cosmology, Divinities], Budge [all books], Kastor, Piankoff [all books]

1.5 Isis: The Image of Atam
Gadalla [Cosmology, Divinities], Plutarch, Budge [all books], Kastor, Piankoff [all books]

1.6 Isis: The Female Re
Gadalla [Cosmology, Divinities], Budge [all books], Kastor, Piankoff [all books]

1.7 Isis: The Dog Star
Gadalla [Cosmology, Divinities], Budge [all books], Kastor, Piankoff [all books]

1.8 The Heart (Isis) Begets The Soul (Osiris)
Gadalla [Cosmology, Divinities], Budge [all books], Kastor, Piankoff [all books]

Chapter 2: The Duality of Isis

2.1 The Duality of Divine Intellect
Gadalla [Cosmology, Divinities], Budge [all books], Kastor, Piankoff [all books]

2.2 The Dual Nature of the Creation Cycle
Gadalla [Cosmology, Divinities], Budge [all books], Kastor, Piankoff [all books]

2.3 The Dual Nature of the Universal Womb

Gadalla [Cosmology, Divinities], Plutarch, Budge [all books], Kastor, Piankoff [all books]

2.4 The Two Ladies and The Diadem
Gadalla [Cosmology, Divinities], Budge [all books], Kastor, Piankoff [all books]

Chapter 3: Isis & Osiris—The Dynamic Duo

3.1 Dualisms in Ancient Egypt
Gadalla [Cosmology, Divinities], Budge [all books], Kastor, Piankoff [all books], Diodorus

3.2 Isis and Osiris as the Solar and Lunar Principles
Gadalla [Cosmology, Divinities], Budge [all books], Kastor, Piankoff [all books], Diodorus

3.3 Isis and Osiris and the four elements of creation
Gadalla [Cosmology, Divinities], Budge [all books], Kastor, Piankoff [all books], Plutarch

3.4 The Societal Role of Isis and Osiris
Gadalla [Cosmology, Divinities], Budge [all books], Kastor, Piankoff [all books]

Chapter 4: The Virgin Mother of 'God'

4.1 Allegory and Fictional History
Gadalla [Cosmology, Christianity], Budge [all books]

4.2 Mary Isis
Gadalla [Cosmology, Christianity], Budge [all books]

4.3 Divine and Immaculate Conception
Gadalla [Cosmology, Christianity], Budge [all books]

4.4 The Virgin Mother of 'God'
Gadalla [Cosmology, Christianity], Budge [all books]

4.5 Mary Isis and Child Refuge Into Egypt
Gadalla [Cosmology, Christianity], Budge [all books]

4.6 The Divine Sacrifice
Gadalla [Cosmology, Christianity, Romany], Budge [all books]

Chapter 5: The Numerology of Isis & Osiris

5.1 The Primary Numbers of Isis and Osiris (2&3)
Gadalla [Harmony, Cosmology], Plutarch

5.2 The Primary Generating Numbers of Shapes and Forms
Gadalla [Harmony]

5.3 The Musical Dynamo—the Generator Musical Fifth—Basis of Harmony
Gadalla [Harmony, Rhythm], Plutarch

5.4 The Binary and Ternary Universal Rhythm
Gadalla [Rhythm]

Chapter 6: Isis' Multitude of Attributes

Budge [all books], Gadalla [Divinities, Cosmology, Harmony, Rhythm, Romany, Christianity], Plutarch, Diodorus, Kastor, Piankoff [all books], Erman

Chapter 7: The Beloved in All Lands

7.1 The Spread of the Egyptian Religion

Budge [Osiris, Gods], Gadalla [Culture, Mystics, Romany, Christianity], Herodotus, Plutarch

7.2 Cosmic Significance of Egyptian Festivals
Gadalla [Mystics, Romany, Christianity], Bleeker, Plutarch

7.3 Queen of Marshes
Gadalla [Mystics, Romany, Christianity], Budge [Osiris]

7.4 Lady of Sorrow—[Cry Me A River]
Gadalla [Mystics, Romany, Christianity], Budge [Osiris], Plutarch

7.5 Isis: Lady of Assumption
Gadalla [Mystics, Romany, Christianity], Budge [Osiris]

7.6 Celebrating Her 'Birthday'
Gadalla [Mystics, Romany, Christianity], Budge [Osiris]

7.7 Celebrating Our (Holy) Mother of the Sea
Gadalla [Mystics, Romany, Christianity], Budge [Osiris], Erman

Chapter 8: The Mighty Heart

8.1 Mary Isis: The Cure-all
Gadalla [Mystics, Romany, Christianity], Budge [Osiris], Diodorus

8.2 Homage to the Queen

Gadalla [Mystics, Romany, Christianity], Budge [Osiris], Gadalla being a native Egyptian.

Appendix 1: Allegory and Egyptian Cosmology

Gadalla [Cosmology, Mystics, Christianity], Bleeker, Plutarch, Diodorus

Appendix 2: The Universal Egyptian Allegory—Isis and Osiris

Gadalla [Cosmology, Mystics, Christianity], Budge [Osiris, Gods], Diodorus, Plutarch

Appendix 3: Heart and Soul—Metaphysical Reflections

Gadalla [Mystics, Cosmology, Christianity], Budge [Osiris, Gods], Diodorus, Plutarch, Shah, Nicholson.

TRF PUBLICATIONS

Tehuti Research Foundation (T.R.F.) is a non-profit, international organization, dedicated to Ancient Egyptian studies. Our books are engaging, factual, well researched, practical, interesting, and appealing to the general public. Visit our website at:

https://www.egypt-tehuti.org
E-mail address: info@egypt-tehuti.org

The publications listed below are authored by T.R.F. chairman,
Moustafa Gadalla.

The publications are divided into three categories:

[I] Current Publications in English Language
[II] Earlier Available Editions in English Language
[III] Current Translated Publications in Non English Languages[Chinese, Dutch, Egyptian(so-called "arabic"), French, German, Hindi, Italian, Japanese, Portuguese, Russian & Spanish]

[I] Current Publications in English Language

Please note that printed editions of all books listed below are to be found at www.amazon.com

The Untainted Egyptian Origin—Why Ancient Egypt Matters

ISBN-13(pdf): 978-1-931446-50-1
ISBN-13(e-book): 9781931446-66-2

This book is intended to provide a short concise overview of some aspects of the Ancient Egyptian civilization that can serve us well nowadays in our daily life no matter where we are in this world. The book covers matters such as self empowerment, improvements to present political, social, economical and environmental issues, recognition and implementations of harmonic principles in our works and actions, etc.

The Ancient Egyptian Culture Revealed, Expanded 2nd ed.

ISBN-13(pdf): 978-1-931446-66-2
ISBN-13(e-book): 978-1-931446-65-5
ISBN-13(pbk.): 978-1-931446-67-9

This new expanded edition reveals several aspects of the Ancient Egyptian culture, such as the very remote antiquities of Egypt; the Egyptian characteristics and religious beliefs and practices; their social/political system; their cosmic temples; the richness of their language; musical heritage and comprehensive sciences; their advanced medicine; their vibrant economy; excellent agricultural and manufactured products; their transportation system; and much more.

Isis : The Divine Female

ISBN-13(pdf): 978-1-931446-25-9
ISBN-13(e-book): 978-1-931446- 26-6
ISBN-13(pbk.): 978-1-931446-31-0

This book explains the divine female principle as the source of creation (both metaphysically and physically); the feminine dual nature of Isis with Nephthys; the relationship (and one-ness) of the female and male principles; the numerology of Isis and Osiris; Isis' role as the Virgin Mother; explanation of about twenty female deities as the manifestations of the feminine attributes; the role of Isis' ideology throughout the world; the allegory of Isis, Osiris and Horus; and much more. This book will fill both the mind with comprehensive information as well as the heart with the whole spectrum of emotions.

Egyptian Cosmology, The Animated Universe, Expanded 3rd edition

ISBN-13(pdf): 978-1-931446-44-0
ISBN-13(e-book): 978-1-931446-46-4
ISBN-13(pbk.): 978-1-931446-48-8

This new expanded edition surveys the applicability of Egyptian cosmological concepts to our modern understanding of the nature of the universe, creation, science, and philosophy. Egyptian cosmology is humanistic, coherent, comprehensive, consistent, logical, analytical, and rational. Discover the Egyptian concept of the universal energy matrix and the creation process accounts. Read about numerology, dualities,trinities, numerical significance of individual numbers thru the number ten; how the human being is related to the universe; the Egyptian astronomical consciousness; the earthly voyage; how the social and political structures were a reflection of the universe; the cosmic role of the pharaoh; and the interactions between earthly living and other realms; climbing the heavenly ladder to reunite with the Source; and more.

Egyptian Alphabetical Letters of Creation Cycle

ISBN-13(pdf): 978-1-931446-89-1
ISBN-13(e-book): 978-1-931446-88-4
ISBN-13(pbk.): 978-1-931446-87-7

This book focuses on the relationship between the sequence of the creation cycle and the Egyptian ABGD alphabets; the principles and principals of Creation; the cosmic manifestation of the Egyptian alphabet; the three primary phases of the creation cycle and their numerical values; and the creation theme of each of the three primary phases, as well as an individual analysis of each of the 28 ABGD alphabetical letters that covers each letter's role in the Creation Cycle, its sequence significance, its sound and writing form significance, its numerical significance, its names & meanings thereof, as well as its peculiar properties and its nature/impact/influence.

Egyptian Mystics: Seekers of the Way, Expanded 2nd ed.

ISBN-13(pdf): 978-1-931446-53-2
ISBN-13(e-book): 978-1-931446-54-9
ISBN-13(pbk.): 978-1-931446-55-6

This new expanded edition explains how Ancient Egypt is the origin of alchemy and present-day Sufism, and how the mystics of Egypt camouflage their practices with a thin layer of Islam. The book also explains the progression of the mystical Way towards enlightenment, with a coherent explanation of its fundamentals and practices. It includes details of basic training practices; samples of Ancient Present Egyptian festivals; the role of Isis as the 'Model Philosopher'.It shows the correspondence between the Ancient Egyptian calendar of events and the cosmic cycles of the universe; and other related miscellaneous items.

Egyptian Divinities: The All Who Are THE ONE, Expanded 2nd ed.

ISBN-13(pdf): 978-1-931446-57-0
ISBN-13(e-book): 978-1-931446-58-7
ISBN-13(pbk.): 978-1-931446-59-4

This new expanded edition shows how the Egyptian concept of God is based on recognizing the multiple attributes of the Divine. The book details more than 100 divinities (gods/goddesses); how they act and interact to maintain the universe; and how they operate in the human being—As Above so Below, and As Below so Above.It includes details of the manifestations of the neteru (gods, goddesses) in the creation process; narrations of their manifestations; man as the universal replica; the most common animals and birds neteru; and additional male and female deities.

The Ancient Egyptian Roots of Christianity, 2nd ed.

ISBN-13(pdf): 978-1-931446-75-4
ISBN-13(e-book): 978-1-931446-76-1
ISBN-13(pbk.): 978-1-931446-77-8

This new expanded edition reveals the Ancient Egyptian roots of Christianity, both historically and spiritually. This book demonstrates that the accounts of the "historical Jesus" are based entirely on the life and death of the Egyptian Pharaoh, Twt/Tut-Ankh-Amen; and that the "Jesus of Faith" and the Christian tenets are all Egyptian in origin—such as the essence of the teachings/message, as well as the religious holidays.It also demonstrates that the major biblical ancestors of the biblical Jesus—being David, Solomon and Moses are all Ancient Egyptian pharaohs as well as a comparison between the creation of the universe and man (according to the Book of Genesis) and the Ancient Egyptian creation accounts.

The Egyptian Pyramids Revisited, Expanded Third Edition

ISBN-13(pdf): 978-1-931446-79-2
ISBN-13(e-book): 978-1-931446-80-8
ISBN-13(pbk.): 978-1-931446-81-5

The new expanded edition provides complete information about the pyramids of Ancient Egypt in the Giza Plateau. It contains the locations and dimensions of interiors and exteriors of these pyramids; the history and builders of the pyramids; theories of construction; theories on their purpose and function; the sacred geometry that was incorporated into the design of the pyramids;

and much, much more. It also includes details of the interiors and exteriors of the Saqqara's Zoser Stepped "Pyramid" as well as the three Snefru Pyramids that were built prior to the Giza Pyramids. It also discusses the "Pyramid Texts" and the works of the great pharaohs who followed the pharaohs of the Pyramid Age.

The Ancient Egyptian Metaphysical Architecture, Expanded Edition

ISBN-13(pdf): 978-1-931446-63-1
ISBN-13(e-book): 978-1-931446-62-4
ISBN-13(pbk): 978-1-931446-61-7

This new expanded edition reveals the Ancient Egyptian knowledge of harmonic proportion, sacred geometry, and number mysticism as manifested in their texts, temples, tombs, art, hieroglyphs, etc., throughout their known history. It shows how the Egyptians designed their buildings to generate cosmic energy; and the mystical application of numbers in Egyptian works. The book explains in detail the harmonic proportion of about 20 Ancient Egyptian buildings throughout their recorded history.It also includes additional discussions and details of the symbolism on the walls; the interactions between humans and the divine forces; Egyptian tombs, shrines and housing; as well as several miscellaneous related items.

Sacred Geometry and Numerology,

ISBN-13(e-book): 978-1-931446-23-5

This document is an introductory course for learning the fundamentals of sacred geometry and numerology, in its true and complete form, as practiced in the Egyptian traditions.

The Egyptian Hieroglyph Metaphysical Language

ISBN-13(pdf): 978-1-931446-95-2
ISBN-13(e-book): 978-1-931446-96-9
ISBN-13(pbk.): 978-1-931446-97-6

This book covers the Egyptian Hieroglyph metaphysical language of images/pictures; the language of the mind/intellect/divine; the scientific/metaphysical realities of pictorial images (Hieroglyphs) as the ultimate medium for the human consciousness that interpret, process and maintain the meanings of such images; how each hieroglyphic image has imitative and symbolic (figurative and allegorical) meanings; the concurrence of modern science of such multiple meanings of each image; how Egyptian hieroglyphic images represent metaphysical concepts; and the metaphysical significance of a variety of about 80 Egyptian Hieroglyphic images.

The Ancient Egyptian Universal Writing Modes

ISBN-13(pdf): 978-1-931446-91-4
ISBN-13(e-book): 978-1-931446-92-1
ISBN-13(pbk.): 978-1-931446-93-8

This book will show how the Egyptians had various modes of writings for various purposes, and how the Egyptian modes were falsely designated as "separate languages" belonging to others; the falsehood of having different languages on the Rosetta (and numerous other similar) Stone; and evaluation of the "hieratic' and "demotic" forms of writing. The book will also highlight how the Egyptian alphabetical language is the MOTHER and origin of all languages (as confirmed by all writers of antiquities) and how this one original language came to be called Greek, Hebrew, Arabic and other 'languages' throughout the world through the deterioration of sound values via 'sound shifts', as well as foreign degradation of the original Egyptian writing forms.

The Enduring Ancient Egyptian Musical System—Theory and Practice, Expanded Second Edition

ISBN-13(pdf): 978-1-931446-69-3
ISBN-13(e-book): 978-1-931446-70-9
ISBN-13(pbk.): 978-1-931446-71-6

This new expanded edition explains the cosmic roots of Egyptian musical and vocal rhythmic forms. Learn the fundamentals (theory and practice) of music in the typical Egyptian way: simple, coherent, and comprehensive.It provides discussions and details of an inventory of Ancient Egyptian musical instruments explaining their ranges and playing techniques. It also discusses Egyptian rhythmic dancing and musical harmonic practices by the Ancient Egyptians and other miscellaneous items.

Egyptian Musical Instruments, 2nd ed.

ISBN-13(pdf): 978-1-931446-47-1

ISBN-13(e-book): 978-1-931446-73-0
ISBN-13(pbk.): 978-1-931446-74-7

This book presents the major Ancient Egyptian musical instruments, their ranges, and playing techniques.

***

The Musical Aspects of the Ancient Egyptian Vocalic Language

ISBN-13(pdf): 978-1-931446-83-9
ISBN-13(e-book): 978-1-931446-84-6
ISBN-13(pbk.): 978-1-931446-85-3

This book will show that the fundamentals, structure, formations, grammar, and syntax are exactly the same in music and in the Egyptian alphabetical language. The book will show the musical/tonal/tonic Egyptian alphabetical letters as being derived from the three primary tonal sounds/vowels; the fundamentals of generative phonology; and the nature of the four sound variations of each letter and their exact equivalence in musical notes; the generative nature of both the musical triads and its equivalence in the Egyptian trilateral stem verbs; utilization of alphabetical letters and the vocalic notations for both texts and musical instruments performance; and much more.

***

Egyptian Romany: The Essence of Hispania, Expanded 2nd ed.

ISBN-13(pdf.): 978-1-931446-43-3
ISBN-13(e-book): 978-1-931446- 90-7
ISBN-13(pbk.): 978-1-931446-94-5

This new expanded edition reveals the Ancient Egyptian roots of the Romany (Gypsies) and how they brought about the civilization and orientalization of Hispania over the past 6,000 years. The book shows also the intimate relationship between Egypt and Hispania archaeologically, historically, culturally, ethnologically, linguistically, etc. as a result of the immigration of the Egyptian Romany (Gypsies) to Iberia.It alsp provides discussions and details of the mining history of Iberia; the effects of Assyrians and Persians attacks on Ancient Egypt and the corresponding migrations to Iberia; the overrated "Romans" influence in Iberia; and other miscellaneous items.

[II] Earlier Available Editions in English Language — continue to be available in PDF Format

Historical Deception: The Untold Story of Ancient Egypt, 2ⁿᵈ ed.

ISBN-13: 978-1-931446- 09-1

Reveals the ingrained prejudices against Ancient Egypt from major religious groups and Western academicians.

Tut-Ankh-Amen: The Living Image of the Lord

ISBN-13: 978-1-931446- 12-1

The identification of the "historical Jesus" as that of the Egyptian Pharaoh, Twt/Tut-Ankh-Amen.

Exiled Egyptians: The Heart of Africa

ISBN-13: 978-1-931446-10-5

A concise and comprehensive historical account of Egypt and sub-Sahara Africa for the last 3,000 years.

The Twilight of Egypt

ISBN-13: 978-1-931446-24-2

A concise and comprehensive historical account of Egypt and the Egyptians for the last 3,000 years.

[III] Current Translated Publications in Non English Languages [Chinese, Dutch, Egyptian (so-called "arabic"), French, German, Hindi, Italian, Japanese, Portuguese, Russian & Spanish]

Details of All Translated Publications are to be found on our website

Made in the USA
Coppell, TX
25 February 2021